Desperately Doodling Debbie

Random Musings on Life, Faith
and Other Brain Boggles

Debra Kuss

WESTBOW
P R E S S®
A DIVISION OF THOMAS NELSON
& ZONDERVAN

Scriptures taken from the Holy Bible, New International Version®, NIV®.
Copyright © 1973, 1978, 1984, 2011 by Biblica, Inc.™ Used by permission
of Zondervan. All rights reserved worldwide. www.zondervan.com The
"NIV" and "New International Version" are trademarks registered in
the United States Patent and Trademark Office by Biblica, Inc.™

WestBow Press books may be ordered through booksellers or by contacting:

WestBow Press
A Division of Thomas Nelson & Zondervan
1663 Liberty Drive
Bloomington, IN 47403
www.westbowpress.com
1 (866) 928-1240

Because of the dynamic nature of the Internet, any web addresses or
links contained in this book may have changed since publication and
may no longer be valid. The views expressed in this work are solely those
of the author and do not necessarily reflect the views of the publisher,
and the publisher hereby disclaims any responsibility for them.

Any people depicted in stock imagery provided by Getty Images are
models, and such images are being used for illustrative purposes only.
Certain stock imagery © Getty Images.

ISBN: 978-1-9736-2169-0 (sc)
ISBN: 978-1-9736-2168-3 (hc)
ISBN: 978-1-9736-2170-6 (e)

Library of Congress Control Number: 2018902456

Print information available on the last page.

WestBow Press rev. date: 06/21/2019

This book is dedicated to Rev. Tim Thompson
the pastor of Grace on the Hill United Methodist Church
in Corbin, Kentucky during the years covered in this book.
Without his invitation for writers for the church newsletter
Desperately Doodling Debbie would have never come into being.
It's all his fault!

In Memory of
my sister
Barbara Violett
and my son-in law's grandmother
Lois Bender
who were my biggest fans.

*The art of writing is the art
of discovering
what you believe.*
-Gustave Flaubert

*Writing has laws of perspective,
of light and shade
just as painting does, or music.
If you are born knowing them, fine.
If not, learn them.
Then rearrange the rules
to suit yourself.*
-Truman Capote

*The difference between
the almost right word
and the right word
is really a large matter.
'Tis the difference
between the lightning bug
and the lightning.*
-Mark Twain

*For we are God's workmanship
created in Christ Jesus
to do good works,
which God prepared in
advance for us to do.*
-Ephesians 2:10 (NIV)

INTRODUCTION

I've been a book nerd from the time I learned to read. As an introverted child, books were my best friends. I discovered the power of the written word when I read Charlotte's Web by E.B. White in the fourth or fifth grade. Until I burst into sobs when Charlotte died and her babies crawled out of their spidery sack, I had never felt the power of a story. I hated spiders and there I was blubbering uncontrollably over the death of one in a book! After that I was forever searching for the next book that would send me into a new world of emotional wonderment.

As I continued through school, I discovered the joy in writing my own tales. English class was the best part of my day, especially when we were given writing assignments. My shy little self enjoyed surprising teachers with the amount of verbiage lurking in my head. As long as I didn't have to speak all those words I was blissfully happy.

In adulthood I've taken whatever opportunities have come my way to write, most of them in church and for poetry contests sponsored by state poetry societies. When Pastor Tim put out the call for people to write for the church newsletter back in 1999, I volunteered. I asked him what he wanted me to write. He said, "Anything you want." So that's what I did! Desperately Doodling Debbie was a column in the church newsletter for seven years. During that time my three daughters grew from ages 15, 11 and 6 to 22, 18 and 13, so most of my writings were about the joys and agonies of parenting. I was working as a secretary for the first couple of years, then moved on to nannying newborn triplets until they were 5-year-olds, so some of that is covered as well.

My grandest dream, other than being a wife and mother, has been to be a published author. KaChing!!

It All Began with a Tightly Wound Christian

April 2000

You may be wondering why in the world this bit of oddness is cluttering up your beloved newsletter. Well, it's simple. Our pastor put out a call for columnists for this new and improved publication, and I, being the tightly wound Christian that I am, said yes! Another opportunity to drive myself insane!

Those of you who are of the same tight persuasion know what I mean. It's just hard to say no sometimes. Especially when there's an element of spirituality to the assignment. And those of us who are tight can find a spiritual significance to just about anything, even nervous breakdowns. (It is so comforting to know we have given our all for the cause of Christ.)

Since we've adopted the theme of "Yes to God!" this year, you may be wondering why I'm not being more encouraging about the "Yes!" thing. Actually I am, in my own convoluted way. The key is to be sure you are saying yes to God, not to the pastor or to a desperate VBS director (although she is praying fervently that God will ask you to volunteer), and certainly not to your own uptight sense of spiritual duty. God has a place for each of us to minister in our church and community. Just be ready with the right answer when He calls.

Here's a promise from God for all of us—for the tight as well as for the loose as a goose. "Let us not become weary in doing good, for at the proper time we will reap a harvest if we do not give up" (Galatians 6:9 NIV).

And for the tight (and those near and dear to them) a special word from me: watch out for the rebound effect when the elastic snaps!

For the Entangled Christian

May 2000

Yes, dear readers, it's time again for your monthly dose of Doodledom. This episode finds me thrashing about in the briar patch with Br'er Rabbit. The only problem is I'm not a rabbit! The more I try to pull myself out of the thorny mesh, the more entangled I become. God calls this being choked by "the worries of this life, and the deceitfulness of wealth" (Matthew 13:22 NIV). I'm not too sure the deceitfulness of wealth has much to do with my problem, but I certainly spend a lot of time yanking at the throttlehold that the worries of this life have on me.

As we learned in last month's column, I'm a tightly wound kind of gal. *Everything* seems of earth-shattering importance to me, even the daily household chores, so I end up wallowing in nervous tension, rather than praising the God who really doesn't care whether I get the toilets clean this week or next. What He does care about is whether I clean them with a good attitude, or not clean them at all in order to spend time doing something more important with a good attitude. My question is this: how many dirty toilets is God going to bless me with before I learn this lesson? If you have the answer, please share it with me. I am sick of dirty toilets.

Here's a poem God gave me to help me keep things in perspective as I battle in the briar patch.

Entangled

My blood streams down, as tangled in the thorns
Of worldly cares I struggle to be free.
But with each desperate pull, there's more of me
Caught in the viny web; impaled and torn,
My blood streams down.

My blood streams down; my cries of pain unheard
By others floundering with me in the maze.
We strain towards life; we strangle in malaise.
Conspiring in this deadly dance, absurd,
My blood streams down.

My blood streams down, as gasping, I appeal
To One outside the fray—His pruners snip,
His hands encircle mine to break the grip
Of barbs too long ignored. And as I heal,
His blood streams down.

For the Squirrelly Christian

June 2000

Another month has come and gone, and once again I have strange thoughts in my head. In case you haven't caught on yet, I'm using this column as my own personal psychotherapy couch, where I let out all the weird stuff on my mind in an effort to be a living illustration of how odd the rest of you aren't. This is called *encouraging my brothers and sisters in Christ*. Just let me know if this is not encouraging to you, and I will quit.

On to the squirrels! When last we met, I was entangled in a thorny toilet. I have moved on from that stinky place, praise the Lord! Now I am twitching nervously on a tree branch. Go figure.

If I Could Fly

If I could fly
like an eagle
high against the clouds
soaring on currents
of unpolluted air,

If I could fly
like a hummingbird
darting bloom to bloom
sipping nectar
deep and pure,

If I could fly
like a spider
floating on threads
to unknown worlds
a few feet away,

If I could fly
I wouldn't be hanging here
like a squirrel
clinging by toenails
to a familiar branch.

Someday I hope to take a flying leap, burst forth into one of my favorite songs, "I Believe I Can Fly" by R. Kelly*, and "soar on wings like eagles" (Isaiah 40:31 NIV). Does that appeal to any other squirrels out there? Just like the Pruner can cut us out of the thorny briars of life, He can also trim our long toenails that keep us clinging to the safe and familiar.

I wonder what would happen if our nation were suddenly invaded by a bunch of flying squirrelly Christians?

---

* TIME WARP: I still like the song, but the singer needs some prayer.

For the Spaced-Out Christian

July 2000

!!!! Tell me I'm not the only one going crazy!!!! Tell me there is life amid the dailyness! Yes, dear faithful readers, I am once again on the edge, about to fall off, but it's not into a toilet or out of a tree this time around. This month I am on the verge of something big. Something Expansive! Something really, really *GARGANTUANLY* **ENORMOUS**! I'm talking about Inner Space, that place in the brain that is left when all meaningful thought has departed to unknown galaxies far, far away.

This abandonment by my own personal brainwaves began, quite coincidentally, around the time of the birth of my third child. The evacuation of headquarters accelerated to warp speed when I hit Deep Space Forty. Now, three years later, with the latest addition to my life—an actual paying job—the blinding light of knowledge that once was mine has disappeared into an ever-growing black hole. This is annoying.

The other day as I was about to pitch a hissy fit at my husband, I was reminded of what Jesus said to Martha when she complained about her sister, Mary, not helping her around the house enough: "Martha, Martha, you are worried and upset about many things, but only one thing is needed. Mary has chosen what is better, and it will not be taken away from her" (Luke 41:10 NIV). Substitute my name for Martha and Bret's name for Mary, and you can visualize the dynamics of the Kuss home when I'm stressing out over stupid things. Bless Martha's heart. I so feel her anguish! She had to live with someone, just as I do, who was calm and peaceful and happy and just plain "BETTER" all the time! Someone with space in the brain for the one important thing—listening to Jesus. Hey, maybe God is the one doing all this mind draining on me these days to make more room for Himself! Perhaps spacy is a good thing to be! I feel a poem coming on.

<u>Midlife Spaces</u>

Quiet chaos
reigns in Deep Space Forty
where old fears collide with new loss,
and shooting pains
crisscross
dark brain matter,
expanding, imploding
while all logical thoughts scatter
with noiseless mind
clatter.
Black holes remain,
sucked full of ideas,
bleak spaces, vacuums, that retain
just the mindless
mundane.
Drafty, lacy
memories vie for room
with the daily, urgent, hasty
No wonder I'm
spacy.

For the Christian in Waiting

August 2000

Once again, I greet you from the counseling couch. Another month, another neurosis! Here's one that's been with me all my life—waiting. For as long as I can remember, I've been waiting for something. When I was a child, it was Christmas. All year long I'd dream about Christmas morning with spine-tingling anticipation. And it took forever to come! (That's one problem I don't have anymore.) Then when the day finally arrived, I would be delirious with joy. After about a week, the waiting would begin for my birthday, only a month later. No wonder Christmas seemed to take forever to arrive!

As I grew up, I waited for school to start, then school to be out, braces to go on, braces to come off, events to come, events to be over. Then came the wait for driving, graduations, marriage, jobs, moving, children. For many years I waited for children to sleep through the night, start talking, start eating regular food, get out of diapers, stop talking so much, stop being so picky about regular food. The list was endless. And now that I've started working in the world again, between waiting for the girls to get through all their myriad year-round activities, it seems I'm constantly awaiting the weekend when supposedly I'll find time to do something more meaningful than washing tons of laundry.

Always underneath it all, I've had the feeling that there's something better, something more—something just ahead, waiting for me. It can be downright exhausting waiting for the unknown! And the worst part is while I'm waiting for the future to get here, I miss a lot of the present. It's that Martha thing again. I get so caught up in preparing for the meal after the meeting that I miss the meeting itself.

What's the answer? Here are a few thoughts:

Sometimes the waiting is part of the process of growing. John Milton, the great 17th century poet, wrote, "Thousands at his great bidding speed and post o'er land and ocean without rest. They also serve who only stand and wait." This guy had just gone blind and thought his life was pretty much over. But Milton must have realized that God was in control and had a reason for this holding pattern he was in. Twelve years later, Milton's *Paradise Lost* and *Paradise Regained* were published. He accomplished a lot during those years of "waiting."

Waiting can be good for us if we're looking forward to the right things. Romans 8:19 (NIV) says, "The creation waits in eager expectation for the sons of God to be revealed," while in Hebrews 9:28 (NIV) we read, "so Christ was sacrificed once to take away the sins of many people; and he will appear a second time, not to bear sin, but to bring salvation to those who are waiting for him." Holy goodness! Jesus is coming back to reveal to the whole universe whom He has adopted with His own blood into God's family. And that's us! Now there's something worth waiting for!

Finally, since we don't know what the next minute holds, much less tomorrow or next month or next year, we need to get out there and live where we are today, because that's all we really have on this earth.

For the Christian with Random Thoughts of Weirdness

September 2000

For the first time since we began this adventure in spiritual neuroses, I find myself with no overwhelming problem to hash out with you. I hope this doesn't disappoint. After all, even the most neurotic among us deserves a moment or two of near sanity. Never fear, however! I have had a couple of random thoughts this month. (Please hold your applause until all thoughts have stepped forward for perusal.)

Random Thought #1 Are we all just facsimiles of ourselves? Up until a few months ago this thought never would have occurred to me. I was blissfully ignorant of that fast paced "fax me!" modern business world. Alas, I am now seriously informed. All day long faxes come and go before my eyes and through my fingers. And as the word implies, these faxes are mere copies of the originals. They contain the same information as the real thing, but a lot of times that information is either too faint to read, or missing the top or bottom line, or even whole pages. They can't be totally trusted to convey the true, full image of the original document.

I don't know about you, but sometimes I don't feel my life conveys the true, full me. I'm not naturally a morning person, but the world's warped schedule forces me to live like one. I'm not naturally interested in anything even remotely connected to the business world, but five days out of the week my thoughts revolve around business. I'm not naturally a nurturing, self-sacrificing person, but for nearly sixteen years I've been a mother. My life represents me, but it is not the real me as I once knew myself to be.

Being a facsimile can be good and bad. It's good that my original self-centered lifestyle has been copied over by the needs of my family. It's not good when the best part of me gets jammed in the machinery of the mundane. Maybe life is just one big facsimile of the one to come. Maybe God was looking at a fax when He inspired Paul to write, "now we see but a poor reflection as in a mirror; then we shall see face to face. Now I know in part; then I shall know fully, even as I am fully known" (I Cor. 13:12 NIV). Someday we will all be our true selves and know each other and God completely!

Random Thought #2 Jesus wept and so have I—over all manner of idiotic things. Besides the normal tear inducing events—deaths, births, weddings, graduations, traffic tickets—why do I find myself getting misty over everything? It started during my first pregnancy, and sixteen years later there seems to be no end to it. In fact, it gets worse the older I get.

At my oldest daughter's first band concert in sixth grade, I teared up over a rousing rendition of "Twinkle, Twinkle, Little Star." As I recall, the band director pulled out his hankie as well. One time at church I cried a fountain over pantomiming clowns. Evidently, they weren't very funny. And I learned to stay away from watching game shows when I had to try to explain to my preschooler why I was crying after an 80-year-old woman won a speedboat on "The Price is Right." Would my daughter understand crying for hilarious joy? No. I told her I was afraid the nice lady would fall out of the boat and drown.

The last straw came a few months ago when we were all watching a nice family video about a boy and his dog. Of course, as in most family movies involving animals, the beloved animal had to go and die at the end. This sent me into paroxysms of weeping for an hour, periodically interrupted by brief moments of lucidity when I would shriek at our dog, "Quit licking yourself!" and "Do you have to breathe so loudly?" This episode confused the children as well as me. My husband, on the other hand, had left the room at the first sniffle.

I don't have a single nugget of spiritual wisdom to share about this crying thing, so count your blessings folks! And whatever you do, don't send me any stories about dogs, children, or game show winners.

For the Peretti-Spooked Christian

October 2000

Once again it is time to delve into our pitifully human psyches and dredge up some fascinating topic for discussion. This month I have chosen to peer into the supernatural world, because frankly, I was more desperate than usual for an idea, so I flipped through my poetry journal until something spiritual appeared. I'm sure a lot of you out there have read some of Frank Peretti's books. I have read only three, because the first one, *This Present Darkness,* gave me such heebie-jeebies I couldn't sleep for weeks. Everywhere I went I was expecting to see demons and angels duking it out over my head. It was several years before I had the courage to read the next one (of which, unfortunately, I cannot recall the title). I do recall, however, that sleep forsook me once again.

For some reason, spiritual warfare frightens me more than murder and mayhem in the streets, maybe because murder and mayhem are a result of the spiritual battles that go on constantly between the forces of good and evil. And even though I know I am on the right side, God's side, the angels' side, I also know how little time and effort I spend in prayerful spiritual warfare, so when evil wins a battle, it is partially my fault for not being more vigilant.

I'm glad I read Peretti's books. Over the years I've thought about them a lot when I've been praying for the safety of my children. More than physical protection, I want them protected from the devil who "prowls around like a roaring lion looking for someone to devour" (I Peter 5:8 NIV). He is so good at disguising himself, children can be lured into his lair right before our eyes. And as evidenced by the many incidents of school violence, that can lead to physical harm for those caught on the battlefield.

That's the story behind the following poem. Even though Satan and his cohorts are scary and devious, God's angels are even scarier for those on the wrong side. Their power comes from God Himself who promises "If you make the Most High your dwelling—even The Lord, who is my refuge—then no harm will befall you, no disaster will come near your tent. For He will command His angels concerning you to guard you in all your ways" (Psalms 91:9–11 NIV). I want these guys standing guard in our schools, businesses and homes. Let's pray to that end.

<u>Vigil</u>
The angels hover, silent, dreadful, calm,
As evil enters, clanging in pursuit
Of one whose heart is weak, in need of balm,
The perfect victim, easy to recruit.
    Flying prayers
    collide with hate
    as battles rage
    unseen
To human eyes. Yet loving hearts know well
The need to keep a vigil, constant, strong.
While laughing children enter school each day,
The angels hover, silent, dreadful, calm.

For Pilgrims in a Strange Land

November 2000

Happy November, loyal readers! I've taken a solemn vow to yank myself out of the muck and mire of mental torment this month in order to honor those great early American settlers, the Pilgrims. Just thinking about them fills me with thanksgiving. I'm thankful they had the courage to leave everything they had ever known to go where they had never been and start a new life. I'm thankful they endured sickness and hardship on the boat ride over and still settled in to persevere through even more problems their first year at Plymouth. And I'm thankful I wasn't one of them, because their lifestyle sounds like a lot of work and misery to me.

And yet they did it, and even celebrated with a feast after their first harvest. So why did they go to all this trouble? Were they just wild and crazy adventurers out for a thrill? Perhaps a few were, but most were searching for a place to explore their faith freely. They were willing to give up the security of the known for the uncertainty of the unknown, because they believed God had something better for them. They chose to act on their faith, and to continue acting on it, even when things didn't seem to be working out all that well, because they knew God wanted them there. They acted according to the vision God had given them of a land where they could worship Him freely, without fear of reprisal from the government or persecution by neighbors. When they arrived, it was up to them to make the vision come to life by the choices they made. Where would we be if they had chosen differently?

Even now, several hundred years later, we must choose to "live by faith, not by sight" (2 Cor. 5:7 NIV) as "aliens and strangers in the world" (2 Peter 2:11 NIV) knowing our God has "plans to prosper (us) and not to harm (us), plans to give (us) hope and a future" (Jeremiah 29:11 NIV). Let us strive to be thankful Pilgrims as we daily choose to make our faith become sight.

The Choice

Hope
assured
but not seen
waits in corners
of the mind for dawn
to reach through louvered blinds
and kiss night-cold eyes of man
awake. To stay in filtered light,
or open shutters wide, is the choice
that determines whether faith becomes sight.

For the Traditional Christian

December 2000

During the holiday season, most of us find ourselves up to our eyeballs in traditions. Each family has a way of "doing" the holidays that makes them special. From the type of Christmas tree we have, to the way we decorate it, from the places we go, to the food we prepare, most of us have been trained from early childhood to expect the celebrations to include certain sights, sounds, and smells. We, in turn, tend to pass down at least some of these traditions to our own children. And when something happens to disturb the pattern of our festivities, our seasonal joy can go right down the tubes.

Growing up, my Christmas was centered around Santa and gifts. Although my parents sent me to Sunday School each week, they did not go to church except maybe on Easter, and Jesus was not mentioned in any positive way in our home. I knew we celebrated the birth of the baby Jesus at Christmas time, but He wasn't a part of our family holiday activities. Christmas was waiting for Santa to come, and later going to grandparents' homes for big meals.

Something happened in 1967, when I was ten years old, to disrupt our traditional holiday. My brother was drafted and sent to Vietnam. That Christmas, for the first time in my life, our family circle was incomplete. It was scary. I began to learn the meaning of prayer.

<u>Rice Paddy Christmas</u>

Gone
beyond
my mind's eye,
I don't know why
my brother tramps through
a jungle of bamboo.
"Why are they fighting, Daddy?"
"Over a stinkin' rice paddy!"
That's all he says, as we wrap presents
while Walter Cronkite, in perfect cadence,
tells us the way it is tonight, Christmas Eve
1967. As if he knows how we grieve.
Bullets fly, bombs explode in technicolor, and I'm
only ten years old and praying for peace at Christmas time.

The next year, our traditions were upended again when we moved from the small town of Warrensburg, Missouri to Kansas City. Since we now lived in the same city as my sister and her husband, they didn't have to come spend the night to be with us on Christmas. And since I was too old for Santa anyway, my mother decided we should have our get-together on Christmas Eve rather than Christmas morning. Talk about taking all the fun out of Christmas! Without the anticipation of waking up to see what Santa had miraculously left for me during the night, Christmas was a sad disappointment for many years.

Christmas Burial

Christmas has changed since I was young,
full of Santa, elves, presents,
and the babe born to die.
Joy-smiles amid bustling crowds
matured into pursed lips.
That special morning's miracles
bursting through torn paper and ribbons
now trickle out politely
after supper on the eve before.
And the babe?
He's buried somewhere
beneath a mountain of gifts,
tinsel and lights,
and the unnurtured faith of a little child.

That could have been my story had I not eventually found that baby buried under all the holiday hullabaloo, discovering a miracle worker even greater than Santa—one who could protect a brother through the horrors of war as well as bless me with a beautiful family of my own, with whom I share old holiday traditions while creating new ones. This Christmas season, no matter what our traditions, let us all make Jesus the center of our celebrations!

For the Terminally Odd—More Random Thoughts of Weirdness

Let's start out the new year right (and century and millennium, for those of you who refused to accept the majority opinion of when the new epoch began last year) with a few well chosen (or just desperately ripped-from-the-brain-at-the-last-second) random thoughts of weirdness.

Random Thought #1 As many of you know, we (meaning the Kuss family) drive to Kansas City approximately once a year. (Every once a decade or so something more exciting comes up for us to do.) Since about 1990 or whenever the Big Quake prediction failed to shake the earth, each time we drive over the Mississippi, I find myself holding my breath, lifting my feet and praying that the New Madrid fault doesn't decide to shift at that moment. The thought of our car flying off a crumbling bridge and plunging headlong into the cold, murky waters of the Big River, while the Arch twists into a new art form, does not thrill me. However, if by some miracle, all five of us could manage to hurl ourselves out of the car, landing on a soft, unquaked riverbank while our car went kersplash, it might be rather fortuitous, since that is most assuredly the only way our vehicle would be rendered so totally unfixable that we would be forced to get something newer and bigger. This would work only if Bret could not find a big enough seine to fish the car out. But I digress.

I might as well move on to **Random Thought #2**, since it is another travel tip. (The first tip, in case you missed it, is to pray and lift your legs whenever you cross the Mississippi.) When traveling north in the winter, check your antifreeze with the little ball thing, and make them float or sink or whatever they do all the way to minus 100 degrees. This will not only keep your radiator from freezing up, but it could keep your marriage out of the frosty zone as well.

Random Thought #3 We attended a burial service while we were in K.C. Bret's sister-in-law's dad died the day after we arrived. He and his family had been a part of our lives since childhood as all of us kids grew up in the same church. Even though it was sad to say goodbye to this faithful man of God, for a few minutes those of us at the cemetery had a kind of New Haven Baptist reunion. We worshipped together again with people we hadn't seen in years, most of whom had moved on from New Haven just as we had. In that cold, quiet place, I caught a glimpse of what heaven will be like when we all celebrate Jesus' gift of eternal life at the ultimate family reunion.

That's all for this month. Contemplate the joys of winter until next time!

For My Fellow Groundhogs

February 2001

Happy February to one and all! You would not believe the trouble I've had trying to think of something even remotely profound to say this month. My brain goes into hibernation this time of year. You'll just have to put up with brainless me until spring, when my life goes into hyperdrive and I am forced to wake up and smell the full stink of life. In my ponderings, I tried to come up with something seasonal to share with you. I dallied with the idea of quoting a Shakespearean sonnet and then segueing into one of my own mushy love poems. But ick! That would be too nauseating for this space. I'll save that idea for an appropriately misdialed fax from work. Hahahahahaha!

That leaves me with Groundhog's Day or President's Day from which to choose. For some reason, after the last few months, with the specter of all those hanging chads on voting ballots dangling over our heads, I'd prefer to contemplate the groundhog. How can such a humble, goofy creature hold the fate of the rest of the winter's weather on his nervous little head? Talk about stress! I don't know why he even bothers to show up at all. It would be much easier for him to stay in his hole and let the world continue guessing along with the Weather Channel meteorologists about what will fall from the sky next. No scary shadows to face, no weird people cheering him on or waiting for a chance to bonk him on the head with a mallet (which is really a fun game if you can find enough groundhogs in a small enough space willing to keep popping up in random sequence). And yet every year Punxsutawney Phil comes through for better or for worse.

Thus, we come, surprisingly and quite randomly, to the spiritual section of this discourse. Aren't we all a lot like groundhogs? (Please hold your gasps of sudden insight. There's no sense in wasting all that breath on someone in hibernation. Save it for spring, when you'll need your every panicked inhalation just to wade through all the activities.) Yes, dear friends, are we not quite content to stay in our warm, safe holes, oblivious to all the weather wreaking havoc on those poor souls out in the world? Isn't it much easier to hide out in our familiar homes and with our favorite fellow groundhogs at church, than to stick our heads out into the shadowy, weather-full world around us? Would we ever venture out of our tunnels if it were not for the example of Jesus, who not only stuck his head out, but traveled on ground level with the whole lot of us for thirty-three years, enduring much worse than a few thwacks with a mallet? Would we manage to venture out without the throng of witnesses surrounding us to silently cheer us past our timidity? Would we notice the masses waiting in the cold for our appearance if they weren't so loud and abrasive in their search for the answer to the future? Wouldn't we simply ignore them and go back to sleep if they were not so annoyingly just outside our door?

Who would have thought the lowly groundhog could give so much pause for thought? The next time I find myself wishing the world would leave me alone, I'll remember Punxsutawney Phil and sneak a peek out of my hole. When I do, I hope I'll look long enough to see the anticipation on the faces of those who do not know what their future holds, and then crawl out among them to lead them to Spring.

Tune in next month for "March Madness—or How Did a Basketball Non-Fan End Up in Kentucky?"

For A Few Brave Souls

March and May 2001

I know I promised you a column about basketball this month, but since I value my life, I won't say much. When Bret first accepted his teaching position at Cumberland College and I was telling a friend in Mississippi that we would be moving to Kentucky, her first response was, "Do you like basketball?" I told her no, totally ignorant of why she would ask such a thing. She said, "You'd better learn to like it!" After living here for twelve years now, I fully understand her comment, but I still do not enjoy basketball. I just nod my head, smiling or frowning according to the look on the person's face when asked the inevitable question that comes my way: "How about that game?" I pretend I know a game was played and empathize to the best of my ability.

Baseball is my kind of sport. You can read a book in the sunshine and look up now and then to see what's happening when you hear the crack of the bat, unless it's the play-offs. Then you need to pay attention to every pitch. In basketball, there's a score or near miss every few seconds and everyone seems to feel the need to scream about each one. This gives me a headache. I'm also not fond of sweaty armpits, but then baseball has its own brand of bodily quirks that I'd rather not go into. What's the point, then? That's what I'd like to know! What is the point of all this sports frenzy?

Here's another question. What's the point of this monthly column?

Debra Kuss

Am I wasting valuable paper with inane ramblings that only a few brave souls read? If so, it's time to say toodle-loo to the Doodle, and leave you all alone. Let me know if I should continue, or I won't be here next month. Either way, whenever you're feeling desperate, even if it's at a basketball game, look to God for help. I'll be reading a book somewhere far, far away.

. . . . .Time Lapse of Two Months. . . . .

To the five of you who responded to my desperate plea for attention in March, be assured that your brave acknowledgment that you do read these wild ramblings saved this column from annihilation at the hand of its creator. Lucky for you, my standards are lower than Abraham's and God's. Five is less than ten, but good enough for me! Thank you, kind souls, for your encouragement! Be aware, however, that these bursts of mental oddness will be briefer. Self-control is a fruit of the Spirit after all.

Now on to the meat of this month's desperate attempt to make sense out of life. Is anyone else out there considering becoming vegetarian? Does this whole mad cow, crazy sheep, and hoof and mouth crud scare anyone else? Lately, when I have a hamburger, I wonder if it will attack my thighs, my arteries or my brain first—or just choke me as I try to swallow the price! The very thought that tiny little blobs of sickness exist that can't be cooked, frozen, washed away or beaten to death makes me ill. Where did these prion things that cause Mad Cow disease come from anyway? Did God create these for some good reason that has gone sour at the hands of man, or have some super spiritual vegetarians been praying for a reason for the world to come around to their way of thinking?

Whatever the case, it's comforting to remember that God knows what He's doing and He has everything under control. We don't have to worry (although we might want to consider our options)

26

about such hair-raising events. God is busy doing what needs to be done to usher in the return of Christ, and we need to be busy doing what He wants us to do to bring souls into His kingdom before it is too late. The next time you grab the opportunity to spend some time with an unsaved friend, offer him Jesus—and maybe a salad!

For the Exhausted

June 2001

Here we are smack dab in the middle of spring (or by the time you read this, nearing the end of spring) and I've missed the whole thing again. "How could you possibly miss this most glorious of seasons, Desperate Doodlebrain?" you may be asking while scratching your curious head.

Being the forgiving person that I am, I will overlook the name-calling and scratching and tell you. For the last six weeks or so I have had my nose buried in a day (and night) planner, scribbling notes furiously as I try to keep up with all the activities running amok within the schools and churches of our fair city, not to mention (though I feel a rabid compunction to mention it anyway) *three spring birthdays* in this family of mine. When my nose has not been buried in the red ink of the calendar, it has been behind the wheel of my car as I've traipsed to and from practices for these events, or it has been snorting at the pain as I shell out money for them, or breathing deeply as I've attended them, or snoring loudly as I've attempted to recover from them. And it's not just my breathtaking nose that's tired. My entire body feels as if it has been pummeled non-stop for two months with one of those big pummeling things the knights liked to use to knock their enemies off their horses. (I'm too tired to try to figure out what those things are called, so just live with it, people!)

Anyway, I know I'm not the only pooped parent/grandparent out there. I've seen a lot of glazed-over eyeballs lately. "Well, what's the solution?" you may ask, without a hint of head-scratching, thank you very much. HOW SHOULD I KNOW? I'M DESPERATE, REMEMBER!!!

This is all I can offer at the moment. We'd better try to enjoy all the excitement while it's happening, because someday these precious fruits of our loins will be out of the house and we'll be left sorting our fruit of the looms for entertainment. Until then, let's not forget to block off some time for God in our busy schedules and teach our children to do the same. After all, someday it will be their turn to schedule and traipse and snort and snore through spring. Won't that be fun to watch?

For the Commotion Concussed

July 2001

Hello fellow desperadoes! It's the day after VBS has ended and I know from past experience that many of you are suffering commotion concussions right now. Your cerebral functions are wacky from a hard blow to the brain. And what's worse, VBS is just one of many continuous jolts that come along almost on a daily basis in this high tech, noisy world. If it's not phones and faxes ringing off their malicious little hooks all day, it's kids screaming, appliances whirring, dogs barking, spouses spouting, cars clunking, parents nagging, televisions muttering, stereos thumping, computers bing-bong bing-bonging, dishes clattering, and bird clocks chirping. And that's on top of all the thinking that goes on in your over-taxed head.

I have one word for you—*SOLITUDE.* It's the best, most glorious remedy for a commotion concussion God ever invented. Somehow, someway, you've got to get away to a quiet place with nobody but God. He's not noisy or nagging. He doesn't thump, mutter, or chirp. He is the great I AM. He just IS! And when you can "just be" along with Him, the mind clears, and the soul is renewed. You can find your true self again, the one God created with delight way back when.

The trick is finding that quiet time and place. This I cannot help you with. You have to recognize your need and want it badly enough to find your way to it. Sometimes that means giving up other things you need or want to do. Or saying no to activities that others want you involved in. But in the long run, getting away from the noise, so that you can hear God's quiet voice on a regular basis, will make you more productive for God's kingdom when you rejoin the cacophony of this world.

And with God in charge, he won't be telling all of us to find our solitude at the same time, so the world and the church won't collapse without us in the midst of the fray every second of every day. Go away and enjoy it!

For Searching Souls

August 2001

I've been doing a lot of searching lately. At work I seem to lose at least one important paper or file every day, so I search desperately until I find it either in the stack of faxes on my desk, in the organizer (where I put it so I wouldn't lose it), on someone else's desk, (where I put it so that person could see it), or sometimes under my rear end, (where I put it for who knows what reason). This is what I call *searching for my long-lost brain.*

Then there's the searching for affordable necessities for my lovely daughters. From midnight madness sales to furniture auctions to paint chip displays to beauty shops to book and music clubs to "scents-o-ramas", I am constantly dragged along on a never ending mad dash to find the perfect outfit, chair, color, hairstyle, sound, and smell that will make each unique young female happy for the next 30 seconds. This is what I call *searching for insanity.*

Recently we've been on a car search. Yes, dear friends, after twelve years of driving the same vehicle, we are venturing into the murky waters of used car shopping. Unfortunately, what we want is not easy to find, so we are traveling all over the countryside looking for an affordable Honda Odyssey minivan that hopefully will last us another ten years. This is what I call *searching for a miracle.*

Finally, this summer I've been on a spiritual search. During my ongoing midlife crisis of ten years and counting, I've been trying to figure out why God ever thought me up. Obviously, He gave me a family to keep going, but is there anything else I'm supposed to be doing along the way? And do I have the time to do it? And the energy? And the faith? This is what I'm seeking to find out in the Sunday School class where we are studying *Visioneering* by Andy Stanley. So far, I wish the class met daily. It is opening my eyes to how God works in bringing about His vision in individual lives. If I do what I know to do at this point in my life, He will take me where I'm supposed to be. This is a search I highly recommend. I call it *searching for the truth that shall make you free.* Yahoo!

For the Parentally Disturbed

September 2001

Here we are again in the back-to-school mode. The smell of new backpacks, paper, pencils, markers, glue, erasers in various colors and scents, socks, shoes, underwear, jeans, stretchy pants, baggy pants, cute tops (that aren't cute enough to make the principal gag, but are cute enough to walk out of the house in), hairspray, gel, spritz, make-up, lunch money, forms to fill out, notices to notice and schedules to fly by—aaahh—the aroma is slightly nauseating. But nevertheless, we forge ahead into another ten months of educational mania. It's enough to make a parent question his/her decision to have children.

Weren't these little creatures supposed to smell of baby powder, spit up and poop forever? Weren't they supposed to scream and squeal alternately for hours and then go to sleep before we did, instead of going out with friends and coming home with friends until way past supper time, which is when we now keel over into our mashed potatoes? Weren't they supposed to give us hours of delight with their unintelligible jabber until we pulled our hair out, instead of challenging our every action with thought provoking (or just provoking) discussions about our complete ignorance of the way life works? Huh? Isn't that what we thought during those first few years of parental bliss? Well, guess what—we were mistaken!

Babies grow up to become people with schedules, responsibilities, and opinions of their own, and we as parents are given the privilege of guiding, nurturing, encouraging, protecting, financing, and loving them along the way. It's a lot like riding a roller coaster—it's wild, scary, exhilarating, noisy, expensive, and constricting. Sometimes we just close our eyes and scream. All along the way, we pray with fervor. And in the end, it's over way too soon. Sometimes it makes us sick, but generally we would recommend it to anyone standing in line to buy a ticket. Why? Because parenting is a God thing, and God things are always way cool. Happy School Year!

For the More Desperate Than Ever

October 2001

<u>Where is God?</u>

When there is terror in the skies
over cities by the seashore
and a little boy dies
that entire towns have prayed for,

When saints in Christ lie in pain
stalked by suffering unrelenting
and children under strain
shoot each other, unrepenting,

When nations wage war in hate
on all who are not like them
and Christian homes are in a state
of constant battle that destroys them,

When lives are ruled by stress and fear
and no one knows which way to turn
where is God?

Where Is God?

WHERE ARE YOU, GOD?

In the silence we will hear Him
Weeping with us
for Paradise lost
and whispering,
"I AM here. I AM the way.
Follow me."

For the Thankful

November 2001

As hard as it is for me to believe, the time has come once again to turn our thoughts toward the holidays. And this year those thoughts are finding stiff competition for brain space amidst the daily news reports of ever more frightening and maddening happenings occurring around the world and right here in our own backyard. That's why I've decided to list a few of the things I'm thanking God for right now and as the holidays approach. If there's one thing that really repulses Satan, it's praise and thanksgiving to God.

My Thanksgiving List for 2001

1. God loves me.

2. Jesus died for me.

3. God is in control.

4. God has already won the war.

5. Corbin is a good place to live in the best country in the world.

6. Pastor Tim and the church staff give their all to the church.

7. The church staff's families support them as they serve in the church.

8. Our church is a loving family of believers.

9. My family is healthy.

10. God meets our needs every day.

11. Many of our country's leaders know God and are striving to follow him.

12. All this craziness is turning people back to God.

13. Our military is working hard to preserve, protect and defend our land.

14. Things could be a lot worse.

Join me in smacking evil upside of the head with a hearty dose of praise to God each day. Happy Thanksgiving!

For the Christmas Crazed

December 2001

Wasn't it just a couple of months ago that we were caroling, shopping, wrapping, partying, baking, carding, traveling and experiencing joyful hysteria over the holidays? Does anyone else think 2001 was the fastest year yet? What has happened to the old 365 days to a year rule? I'm sure this one had maybe 72 days in it. But enough of my holiday whining! As a devout Bapodist (half Baptist, half Methodist), I don't believe in partaking in whine—although right now a little NyQuil sounds pretty good. I digress.

The point to this column, believe it or not, is to fill you with holiday cheer for a brief moment, before you leap headfirst and fully clothed into the swirling madness around you. Obviously, I have already leapt. I am in full holiday alert mode. I know exactly how many shopping days are left (not enough), how much money is left (way not enough), and how many hours it will take me to complete the cheerful tasks before me (more than any human being can squeeze into the next few weeks).

That's why I am calling it all off! **There will be no Christmas this year!** Take down your trees, put away your credit cards, cancel your travel plans, turn off your oven, stuff your wrapping paper under your bed, curl up with a book and enjoy all your freed-up time.

Wait a minute. That's a bit drastic, I suppose. So instead, here's my suggestion (and I hope I'm listening). ***Look at your Holiday to do list and slash something off it.*** The entire world does not need homemade candy from your kitchen. Every person you've ever known does not need a homemade Christmas card and two-page letter from you. Your children do not need to find their every heart's desire under the tree on Christmas morning. Every holiday happening does not have to have you personally in attendance in order to be a success. Find something on your list that you can do without and do without it this year. And with the free time you give yourself, give Jesus a gift of some stress free, heartfelt praise. That will make the Christmas season truly joyful.

Just don't slash me off your list. I like all those candies and cards. (This is a parting joke to make you chuckle. Go ahead and slash away!)

For the Dizzy of Brain

January 2002

Long time devoted readers, and those who are joining me for the first time in my desperate attempt to make sense of this sojourn on earth—howdy and Happy New Year! As a change of pace from the hectic times we have just lived through (which in reality I am still experiencing at this moment, because I am writing this two days before Christmas so you can read it in your now) I have decided to give you some time to reflect and ponder in this most glorious of all reflective and ponderous months.

This will also save me a little effort in my own time warp (the near past to you, but to me the very present present—yes that's two presents for me!) which is, if you think about it, quite convenient for both of us. This gives me some time off, while you enjoy a little peace, a little silence in the midst of noisy chaos, a little down time when voices are calling you to get back to work. And here's the neatest part—your little moment of nothingness may last as long as you like, since there's no real rule that I know of regarding the length of white space on a page in relation to how long it should take to get through it. If you're a speed reader, you may want to slow down now. This is your big chance to say to someone trying to push you back into the swing of things, "Hey, I'm reading! When I finish I'll get on with life." So here goes—my after-Christmas gift to you:

Thank me now (for you) and later (for me). I'll see you when our time lines converge!

For Valentines and Other Mushy Creatures

February 2002

Last year I avoided the obvious February theme by writing about the oft maligned groundhog. This year I bow to convention and take on the subject of romance by offering you, my faithful readers, a couple of heartfelt love poems. Snuggle up with your sweetie-buns and relive the thrill of new love:

<u>Fly-By Shooter</u>

Stupid
Cupid
shoots his darts
willy
nilly
into hearts,
blinding,
binding
souls diverse.
Fly-by
sly guy--
How perverse!

And specially dedicated to the one I love, Dr. Kuss, fan of all things amphibian and reptile:

Amphibian Melody

Croaking with love
on rain-slicked roads
frogs sing the blues.
Puffed up with pride, they're sometimes caught
or squished by cars, but when love calls,
Frogs sing the blues.

For the Winter Weary

March 2002

This has been a weird winter. With temperatures bouncing around between the 20's and the 70's from week to week and sometimes from day to day, it has been difficult to acclimate to the cold weather when we've had it. I've gone from shivering under blankets in the morning to fanning myself in the afternoon and back to shivering in the evening. Such goings on are hard on a body.

Sometimes the same thing happens to me spiritually. I seem to go from warm (full of faith and positive thoughts) to cold (sure my life is a total pit of doom) in a matter of seconds. That's hard on a body, too— and a mind and spirit. What's the answer to my annoying roller coaster of a spiritual life?

Maybe I should approach it as I have the weather this winter. When Satan blows his cold wind my way, telling me my life is worthless or God is sick of me, I need to grab a spiritual blanket really quick before I pass out in the snow and die of hypothermia. Now what would make a good spiritual blanket? (You people are ahead of me here, I'm sure.) God's Word, of course! Even though I know God loves me and has blessed me and has only good gifts waiting for me to open, I need to be reminded of this on a daily basis. I need to shut out the weathermen (other people) shouting their constantly changing and contradictory forecasts and advisories at me, hover under the blanket of the Bible, and let God create a little Spring in my shivering heart. And because God is never-changing, His blanket can continue to keep me warm after I have to crawl out from under it and go about my business in the cold world. Here's a little poem to get you in the mood for both kinds of Spring.

In Spring

when baby robins sing
and tulips blossom pink and red
the frost is shed
from winter weary souls
whose only goals
of late have been
to see the sun again
and beat the drum
anticipating days to come
when baby robins sing
in spring.

For Spinning Racers

April 2002

Hey, gang! It's time for another installment of "As the Doodle Spins." T.S. Eliot once wrote, "April is the cruelest month," and I think I might agree. It's the month when the world starts spinning out of control around our house, as we careen from one activity to the next in an ever more dizzying race toward the end of the school year. For those of you who have no children, or whose children are all grown up, or whose children do not control your lives because you are smarter than the rest of us—go ahead and laugh at the plight of those of us entering The Big Race. But please pray for us as well. We will survive, and you don't want us coming out of our crazy season any grumpier than necessary.

Since my brain is doing cartwheels at this moment, I really have nothing much to say other than "Thank God for triplets!" Yes, I've started my new career in Mommy Facilitation at the home of some fellow church members and it is a delight beyond words. Babies are so much more fun and worthwhile than stinky paperwork. Even if they do make the body tired and the brain spin!

Here's a poem about this phase of life I'm in.

Attention Relegation Disorder

My mind is weary of thinking so much;
The whirring deafens within me
All other sounds competing to touch
The core of my attention.

When I was younger, the noise stayed outside;
My thoughts streamed both brilliant and free
From some inner place, where I could abide
Without all this contention.

Now with a life full of family and work,
The spirit of "me" hides away
Under urgent chores that I must not shirk,
Fulfilling obligation.

Perhaps in old age, once children are grown,
Bold thoughts will emerge from the fray,
Wiser and kinder, like seeds to be sown,
Matured by relegation.

For the Randomly and Systematically Weird

May 2002

For all of you who have fried brains and mushy bodies, here are a few easily digestible random thoughts of weirdness to tide you over until the next full-course meal of wisdom (which you'll have to find in someone else's column).

Random Thought #1 In Ecclesiastes 3:1 (NIV) we read, "There is a time for everything, and a season for every activity under heaven." That little gem of insight has been oh so brilliantly played out in my life the last few weeks. I was blissfully helping with the little triplets, thinking what a grand life I had playing with babies for eight hours, then going home to my own children, who can pretty much take care of themselves, and who sleep through the night (and halfway through the day when given the chance), when kersproing! Sunny the Golden Retriever dropped a set of newborn bunny triplets in my lap and my cushy life took a shocking nosedive! Suddenly, I was up every three hours feeding kitten formula from a medicine dropper to these tiny creatures, cleaning bedding every day, and worrying whether I was caring for them properly. After two 24-hour periods of this non-stop parental hovering I was exhausted, crabby, and wishing those bunnies would turn into teenagers. Obviously, I had lost all rational thinking skills. Anyway, I heard a little chuckling voice in my head saying over this turn of events, "Enjoy every season

God gives you, Debbie. There's no going back, and if there were, it would kill you." (By the way, at this writing, the bunnies are thriving and will soon be ready to go somewhere—Aack! Another parenting trauma on the horizon!)

Random Thought #2 How come scientists (especially one certain Biology professor) see nothing wrong with letting nature have its cruel way with helpless, abandoned baby critters, and therefore sleep peacefully through the night?

Not so Random Thought #3 How come am I not a scientist?

Until next month, ponder these questions, and avoid all retrieving dogs.

For the Tizzified Traveler

June 2002

Ah, the rejuvenating joys of June! School is out. Musicals, recitals, banquets, field trips, concerts, programs, talent shows, major-last-minute-gotta-get-this-knowledge-crammed-in-before-the-year-ends projects and finals are over. Grades are in. It's time for some rest and relaxation!

But alas, many of you out there are gearing up for VBS (which is a good thing) or you are scrambling to get out of town on the annual trek to wherever (also a good thing). The trouble is, although both of these venerable summer activities are good, they tend to be quite exhausting. Preparing for a trip or preparing for VBS each causes much mental strain and physical anguish, what with all the list-making, stuff-collecting, and oh-mercy-I'd-better-get-this-done-beforehand doing. In other words, we tend to work ourselves into a full-blown tizzy, so that when the anticipated event finally breaks upon us in all its flurry of fun and excitement, we are already dizzy with weariness.

This year I am in a bigger tizzy than usual. Even as you read this I am either preparing to, or in the process of, leaving the country (and I don't mean just the backwoods of Kentucky—I mean the dear old U.S.A.!) Daughter Amy and I are traveling with a group from Corbin High School on a whirlwind tour of parts of northern Europe and Great Britain. We have saved our pennies for four years to be able take this trip and terrorists will just have to get out of our way! As a mother leaving two children and a husband behind, and as a reluctant flier no matter what the circumstances, my tizzy level is at an all-time high. I don't want to sleepwalk through all these places I've wanted to see for as long as I can remember, due to sleep-deprived or Benadryl-induced zombiosis, so here's the deal. I promise to pray for all you dear souls who are giving of yourselves to the children of Corbin during VBS even while I tromp around the streets of Europe. Would you please pray for Amy and me while you tell stories, cut, paste, color and sing?

Maybe we can all help each other quell the Dizzy Tizzies so that we can enjoy the frenzy!

For the Intensely Thrilled Traveler

July 2002

Guten Tag, Bonjour, Hallo, Hello and Howdy all the way from the sunny streets of Corbin! Yes, Amy and I have returned from our twelve-day, 12,735 mile (roughly figured from a children's atlas) whirlwind tour of six countries way yonder across the Atlantic. Here are a few quotes from my fomenting brain during the journey. (If you'd like the minute by minute playback of the trip, ask me when you have several days to kill.)

1. "Yikes! I'm flying over the ocean!"—over the Atlantic

2. "Wow! I can't believe I'm here!"—everywhere, except Knoxville.

3. "Good heavens!"—viewing the sights in we're -not-in-the-Bible-belt-anymore-Amsterdam

4. "Ooh, look at the cows and sheep and canals!"—countryside in the Netherlands

5. "Ach! Mein homeland!"—Germany

6. "Hmmm. Lace, chocolates and a statue of a wee-weeing boy!"—Brussels, Belgium

7. "Ooh la la! C'est Paris! This is way too incredible!"—Paris, mais oui!

8. "Run for your life!"—crossing the streets in Paris

9. "The French I learned years ago in America really does sound similar to what these people are speaking, only this is for real!"—Paris

10. "Ick!"—crossing the churning English Channel by hydrofoil boat

11. "What odd traditions!"—watching the Palace Guards parade around in London

12. "Look at all the famous dead people!"—Westminster Abbey, London

13. "Suck it in and hold on!"—tiny sleeping car on train to Edinburgh, Scotland

14. "Watching men in skirts, blowing into squealing air bags, makes for some fine entertainment while eating haggis!"—Scotland

15. "Gorgeous countryside. Bret would really like it here!"—Scottish Highlands

16. "How do you flush this toilet?"—everywhere

17. "I'm exhausted. Let's start saving for the next trip!"—home

18. "God is good!"—all the time and everywhere

Until next month, when perhaps I'll think of something more spiritual to say.

For World Traveling Home Improvers

August 2002

Have you ever noticed how brilliant ideas that come to you while you are thousands of miles from home in an extravagantly go-for-it frame of mind tend to tarnish rapidly when you return home and need to actually act upon your former brilliance? Or if they don't tarnish, they certainly cause major disruptions in the summer tranquility aura that you have so looked forward to for months? If not, let me tell you what happened to me, so perhaps you'll keep your brain engaged while enjoying the thrills of other-worldliness.

I traveled to Paris, bought some little Monet prints at the Louvre and told Amy, "These are going to be the focal point of our master bedroom renovation just like on "Trading Spaces." (If you don't know about "Trading Spaces," don't watch TLC on weekdays at 4:00 or Saturdays at 9:00—unless you can control your inner decorator.) Then I found a woolen scarf in Edinburgh that matched the pretty blues and greens in the prints, and voila! A total "Trading Spaces" room makeover was practically complete! Except for all the work.

Unfortunately, I missed out on the whole paint and build stuff gene. (I tend to slop paint where it doesn't belong and trip over dust mites hurling me into carefully crafted décor, so I'm banished from doing much in the home project realm of life.) Lucky for me, Bret has great construction worker DNA. That's how come we are no longer floating along on a tranquility aura. Since it took us a month to agree on paint color, and since one idea leads to another, we (I heard that snort, Bret) are now involved in a massive project of building bookshelves, headboard, blanket chest, and shutters, finding bedding, arranging and rearranging around wet walls, washing windows, and periodically glaring at each other. (He glares at me because I am inept, and I glare at him for having the gall to glare at me when I'm just trying to create a restful atmosphere for him to come home to whenever he finally goes back to school!) And that's another problem. My whole brilliant idea will be ruined if we don't do something about the rest of the lame house!

And so, dear readers, here's the spiritual nugget you have been waiting for, lo these many paragraphs: "Husbands, love your wives. . ." (Eph.5:25 NIV) even when they desert you for two weeks only to come home bursting with brilliance that will ruin your summer and possibly the rest of the year. "And wives, submit to your husbands" (Eph. 5:22 NIV) even if it means you're not allowed to do anything but roll on the primer paint. Isn't it amazing how well God planned out this whole marriage deal? (I'm trying really hard not to laugh hysterically right now as my sweet husband groans while applying glorious blue swirly paint to our walls.)

For the Parched Christian

September 2002

Dearest Readers, as much as we may hate it, we must say goodbye once again to the season of travel, home improvement projects, and other stress inducing frivolity. It's time to get back to the serious stresses of life in the fast lane! But before leaving summer in the dust, I feel a deep need to inflict one final poetic thought upon you. Even though we've had some rather hot weeks this year, we've also enjoyed a number of refreshing rains along the way. What a relief it is when a summer shower blows in to cool us off and water the dry ground. For children (and perhaps some adults) these downpours provide the perfect setting for carefree dancing and playing.

God often rains on our parched souls in the same way. We may feel as the psalmist did when he wrote, "As the deer pants for streams of water, so my soul pants for you, O God. My soul thirsts for God, for the living God. When can I go and meet with God?" (Psalm 42:1-2 NIV). It is at these times of spiritual dryness and longing that God will often surprise us with an invigorating shower straight from heaven. Let's strive to always be ready to dance in His rain.

Debra Kuss

As Summer Rains

As summer rains refresh the land
Reviving us from sun baked haze
We sense the gentle, loving hand
Of One who knows our driest days.

We look to Him to clear the ways,
As summer rains refresh the land,
And lead us through the world's mad craze
To quiet spots beyond the strand.

Though sometimes mired in shifting sand
And struggling to retain His gaze,
As summer rains refresh the land
He guides us where our souls may graze.

Tomorrow, through whatever maze
We face unknowns and take a stand,
His presence any fear allays
As summer rains refresh the land.

For Those with No Desire
to Read a Column

October 2002

This glorious month of October, my favorite month of the year, finds me with so many thoughts whizzing around in my head that I can't think of anything coherent to say. Therefore, I've decided to make a list of my thoughts and let you, the most blessed readers, congeal them into some semblance of order. When you have succeeded in writing my column for me, please turn it in to the church secretary for next month. This will save me some brain strain while transforming this column into a state-of-the-art spiritually nuggetizing interactive family entertainment piece. And that's not something that just anybody could or would want to say!

Okay, here we go. Connect these thoughts into something that makes a profound and yet enjoyable point:

1. Nineteen years ago, I was praying that God would bless us with a little girl in October of the next year. Eighteen years ago, on October 1st, Amy Beth was born.

2. Thirty-eight years ago, I saw the Beatles on the Ed Sullivan show for the first time. I've been a fan ever since. Now I'm going to go see Paul in concert for the first time on October 5th! Pray that I won't faint, because the seats are way up high.

3. I'm glad God thought up trees with leaves that change color in the fall.

4. I'm the mother of an eighteen-year-old!

5. Life makes me tired.

6. What's the point of gray hair anyway?

7. She's going away to college in less than a year.

8. Our bunny escaped into the woods. Even the dog is sad.

9. I'll still have two girls at home for a while.

10. The Bible says to rejoice in the Lord always.

11. Yeehaw! God is good.

With a Little Help from My Friends

November 2002

The last time we met here in the pages of this venerable publication, I was so psychologically scattered that you had to write your own column from my drivel. Well, guess what! This month I have come to grips (for the moment) with the impending leave-taking of my eldest daughter. I've newly refurbished the brilliance of my graying locks (Sun In, people!), and I'm basking in the nuclear glow of my first Paul McCartney concert. Bliss and restlessness are now at war in my soul.

Up to this point, 2002 has been one excitement/mental swirl after another. From preparing to visit Europe to actually going, from having no more babies to having triplets to enjoy without the accompanying parental responsibilities, from anticipating Paul to actually soaking in his essence with 18,000 other people, I've experienced two major life dreams, plus one I never would have thought up on my own, in just a matter of months. God has outdone Himself (even though that must be impossible). Now I must deal with the everyday humdrumness of life again (except for the babies who are getting more exciting all the time). And I must do it with an outward normalcy lest my family and employers ship me off to the not-so-funny farm for middle-aged gypsy/groupie-wannabes. Therefore, in the spirit of thanksgiving for such a blessed year, and because you, dear readers, have been so kind as to listen to these pathetic rantings, I dedicate the following to all of you who keep me sane with your kindness and prayers.

My Compass

My spirit yearns to wander like a hound
In search of sights and scents beyond my ken.
And then just as I think that what I've found
In some exotic spot where I have been
Will lend enough adventure to my heart
To satisfy the hunger growling there,
I sense another longing rip apart
The momentary joy of being where
I've never been before. And so I'm lost.
Within a maze I follow my rogue nose
Around the world no matter what the cost
Until my compass leads where friendship grows.
For after all the places I may roam
My spirit sings at sights and sounds of home.

Or in the words of one of my favorite poets (Paul!!!), "the long and winding road…always leads me here, leads me to your door." Let's all get back and let it be!

For People Who Enjoy Non-Existent Words and Really Long Sentences

December 2002

Happy Advent, Merry Christmas, Happy Birthday Jesus! Yes, that most blessed of seasons is upon us yet again, and my thoughts have moved on from Paul McCartney (whom I am not going to mention even once in this meandering column for the rest of the year—oops—well, at least not after this sentence ends, if it ever does) to more spiritual pursuits, such as finding my lost sanity underneath all the wrapping paper that has nothing to wrap itself around as of yet.

In reality, pursuing my sanity is not all that spiritual an adventure, since if I were truly spiritual I wouldn't be insane (or at least not this insane). Let me share with you this little epiphanous thought that came to me the other day in the midst of my seasonal tizzification. I was hyperventilating over my holiday to-do list (which can be very dangerous unless you happen to write your to-do list on a paper bag, which I don't) when the thought came to me, "Christmas is coming! Christmas is coming and I can't stop it!" This brilliant Paul Revereish warning jangling in my brain led to the thought, "Whoa, Nellie!" (Nellie is my sane self, by the way.) "Doesn't Advent mean 'coming'?"

And Nellie thoughtfully answered, "Yes, so what?"

"So what?" I(nsane me) said. "This is the Advent season. We're supposed to be looking forward to, preparing for, and totally getting ourselves ready for the Coming!"

Nellie rolled her eyes at I(nsane me). "Yeah, well that's what I would be doing if you would just leave me alone, and let me get to this list you just hyperventilated at me."

"But Nellie," I(nsane me) said, while patting her poor, deluded sane head. "Think about it. That list was concocted by I(nsane me). I(nsane me) is preparing for the wrong thing. I(nsane me) is getting ready for 'Christmas is coming! Christmas is coming!'"

"Yes, Lulu," (Nellie's kind pet name for I(nsane me.)) "That's what we're all getting ready for this time of year."

"But shouldn't we be preparing for 'Christ is coming! Christ is coming!' instead? It is His birthday after all. Isn't it more important to have hearts that are ready to celebrate His coming, than to have decorated houses and gifts and food and parties?"

"Hmmm," Nellie hmmmd. "That makes sense. But what do I do about this list you made?"

"Whenever you come to something on the list that makes you think more about Christmas than Christ, just say, 'This is not Advent-ageous to me, and don't do it, or at least tone it down so you can see Christ in it."

"Lulu," Nellie said, "you may be crazy, but I don't know what I'd do without you."

"Right back at you, sister!"

For Nellie and Lulu Fans

January 2003

When last we entered inside this Desperada's mind, the Cerebralspasm sisters, Nellie and Lulu, were raucously discussing the whole Christmas/Advent season, quite rudely interrupting all other possible thoughts I may have enjoyed thinking had the girls not been so loud. Suffice it to say, we all made it through that most harrowing of peaceful holidays with nary a hair out of place (all hair yanked out in stress mode remains on the carpet until it becomes advantageous to vacuum—sometime in March, perhaps).

Anyway, now the "gag me sisters" are arguing about New Year's resolutions of all things. Why don't they just hush and let me rest?

"How many resolutions are you making this year, sis?" Lulu asked.

"None! If I make them, I'll break them," sensible Nell answered. "Are you making your usual twenty-nine?"

"No, I've decided to really go for it this year and try for thirty!"

Nellie snorted and chortled. "You know you won't keep them. You never do. Why put yourself through all that guilt and despair?"

"Nellie, I think it's important that I at least give it a shot to improve myself for as long as I can stand it," Lulu said. "After all, maybe this year I'll make it to February."

"Wait a minute, Lulu! I just had a raving mad thought, similar to the ones you entertain in your basement now and again. Maybe we're making the wrong kind of resolutions. We shouldn't be trying to improve ourselves."

"Oh, I get it, Nello! We should resolve to be worse than we are right now, so when we fail, we'll actually succeed at improving! You're a genius!"

"No, you're a loony bird, Lulu. That's not what I meant at all. What we need to do is resolve to let the Lord improve us. He never fails."

"Whoa, Nellie! That's way deep in profundity. I think I'll try it. But what do I do with my list of resolutions?"

"Pray about them and let God tell you which one or two to concentrate on. Then ask Him to help you do whatever needs to be done."

"High five me, Sis! You've hit the nail into my head."

No wonder I have a headache.

For Brrrr Chilly Shivering Winter Weary Souls

February 2003

Hey peoples! I'm baaaack! Nellie and Lulu, my half-brained mental soul sisters, have entered into hibernation for a few moments, so I'm going to try to restrain the inner weirdness and go a little deeper. To me, that means a poem, so I'm going to get to the point and make it snappy!

We're in the depths of winter. I like winter, the snow and cold frosty air, but along about mid-February, I'm tired of counting goose bumps for entertainment. I'd rather count flowers. Serving God can feel the same way. There comes a time when we're just tired of what we've been doing. We're cold and bored. We want to move on to a more vibrant season. The trouble is we're not in charge of the seasons. God is. And He says, "Let us not become weary in doing good, for at the proper time we will reap a harvest if we do not give up" (Galatians 6:9 NIV). Let's press on, then, making bouquets from flowers He sometimes sends in the midst of winter.

<u>Winter Warriors Unaware</u>

We saw them
through gray branches--
bobbing splotches of yellow,
daffodils dancing
a spring jig
in unnatural February warmth.
We picked bouquets,
careful to leave some for others,
dreaming of days to come
with tulips and irises
and wading in creeks.
We hurried home
to place them in vases
all over the house,
sunny promises
to wake up to.
We slept deeply,
the day of outdoor play
exhausting.
We woke to find
mounds of snow
covering the ground,
tiny specks of icy
sunshine peeking through
under the trees.
We were heroes,
our daffodils
fair maidens,
saved from the dragon's
frosty breath.

For the Lentless Among Us

March 2003

By the time you read this, we will be entering the season of Lent once again. Since I grew up in a Baptist church, Lent was never something I pondered very deeply. I thought it was just one of those odd rituals Catholics followed that had nothing to do with me. After all, I was a Baptist, and Baptists didn't do rituals—except for fun stuff like "walking the aisle," getting baptized as many times as it took for it to be a true "believer's baptism," going to church every time the doors were open, going on visitation even if the visited had to do all the talking (because nothing ever seemed to come out of my mouth after "Hi!"), Christmas time Lottie Moon Foreign Missions and Easter time Annie Armstrong Home Missions offering campaigns and studies, with of course, the occasional potluck thrown in for a good fellowship. With all that going on, who had time for something as mysterious as Lent?

Nine years ago, however, something happened. The always and forever Baptist Kuss family joined a Methodist church and found out that we were suddenly a part of the Lent-doing crowd. What a shock! The first couple of years I just sat back and tried to figure out what Lent was all about. I avoided the Ash Wednesday service because it seemed too odd. Then my daughters started coming home with smudges on their foreheads every year and I thought, "My mercies! They think this is normal. They must be real Methodists!" They also started giving up things for Lent and actually sticking it out for the entire season. I tried fasting at lunch time one year, and found that instead of thinking more about Jesus, I just thought more about food. Since then I have spent most of the Lenten seasons trying to decide whether I should give something up and if so, what could I give up that wouldn't end in complete, guilt ridden failure. And I still avoid Ash Wednesday—I'm usually not feeling well, or what's closer to the truth—lame.

Why am I confessing all this to you, dear readers? I don't really know. I guess I'm starting my yearly guilt trip early. Here's the real crux of the matter: since we've been reciting the Apostles' Creed nearly every Sunday, I've been thinking more about the whole denominational issue. The true church is made up of all people who believe those doctrines in the Creed, no matter what rituals they follow or don't follow. The only "follow" that really matters is following Jesus. As long as I do what He wants me to do, I don't have to worry about whether ashes ever touch my head, or how many days I can go without chocolate. If he leads me to do something I've never done before, He will strengthen me to see it through. And if He isn't leading, then I don't have to feel guilty.

Hey! That's where I'm starting this year for Lent. *I'm giving up guilt.* Maybe I'll see you in the line for ashes—or maybe not.

For Faith Wanderers

April 2003

Help! Is there anyone out there who feels lost in a maze of events, paperwork, chores and mind-cluttering details that never seem to end, but instead, reproduce themselves with annoying fertility every time you dare to lift your weary head from the hard, cold table where it plunked with a thud the last time you remember thinking a coherent thought? Or is it just me? (Please say "No, it's not just you, Debbie. Life really is that exhausting!" Otherwise, I will be really depressed.)

Here's the next question. Why must we live this way? Aha! I have an answer for that one. If life were not so complicated, we could breeze through it on our own little steam engine, pulling a sleeper car for God just in case we happen to need Him. Hmmm. Wait a minute. On second thought, maybe that's what we are doing—running back and forth from the engine to the sleeper, trying to wake God up and get Him to take over every time we're headed for a wreck. ("Hey, God! Wake up! There's a bridge out ahead. You need to do something! Quick! Yoohoo! We have like ten seconds here!")

My final question is this—why is it easier to trust God with the really big stuff ("It's war, God. Your turn.") or the little piddly details ("I'm tired of this junk, God. I'm off to the sleeper for a while. Wake me, when I need to do something.") than it is to trust Him with the medium items, that are important to us, but not really life or death issues ("She wants to go to a college that is not on our tuition exchange list. It's a great school, but we can't pay for it. You're going to have to do something, God. Why are you prying my hands off the wheel? Don't you see that big gaping money canyon ahead? I need to use evasive action to keep my daughter from falling into that or I'll be a bad parent! How am I supposed to just trust you with that?")

I think I'll go to the sleeper for a while and rest. Thinking about that last paragraph and trying to punctuate it has done me in. God's a better parent and punctuator than I am. He can handle it.

For Commencing Parents

Another whirlwind school year is gearing up to wind down, and I'm commencing to commence into another phase of parenthood. Although Bret and I will continue parenting as in the past with two of our children, we will be moving on to uncharted waters with another. But that's the way it has been since the day Amy was born. Everything has always been uncharted territory with her, while with the other two, we've been there, done that (until one of them decides to act un-Amy-like just to throw us off, which happens only every other day or so).

What then, is my convoluted point, anyway? I guess I'm saying that from the moment that squirming little bundle of joy pops out until he or she moves out or we poop out, parenthood is all about commencing. Nothing stays the same. No matter what we do as parents, our little progenies are always throwing something new at us.

Because I tend to be somewhat forward thinking, this whole graduation thing has been looming before me like a dreaded wild beast waiting to pounce upon my sentimental head for about eighteen years now. I think I'm ready to just get the mauling over with and move on.

But first, for you other commencing parents out there, let me leave you with a tiny poetic thought that came to me one day when Amy was a short, cutie-pie two-year-old, acting exactly like a short, not-so-cutie-pie two-year-old. Happy May!

Like Daughter, Like Mother

Tugging
my skirt,
her face turns up
in hope
and whining
desperation
for a candy,
the feast served
fifteen minutes earlier
forgotten,
toys
given in love
strewn
carelessly
on the floor.
Now I know how God feels.

For Women with Men to Appreciate

June 2003

By the time you read this, the custodial crew at Corbin High should have finished mopping up the puddle that once was me left behind on the gym floor after graduation. It's time to move on to other desperate subjects.

Since this month we celebrate Father's Day, let's just charge right into the most desperate of all topics known to women—men. But before you get all juiced up for a bash party, let me assure you that this is not the forum for that. After all, this is a church newsletter, and God did invent the whole idea of maleness, so we must agree that God surely knew what He was doing. Therefore, I would like to remind all of us girls that we need to show whatever special men we have in our lives, whether fathers, husbands, boyfriends, brothers, sons, nephews, uncles or friends, some extra appreciation this month, no matter how much they may drive us crazy at times.

For me, that means my dear husband. I'm sure those of you who know him think that he is just an all-around nice guy, of whom I could never, ever find fault. And you would be right about him. Unfortunately, you would be wrong about me, because as a not so nice female, I manage to find fault with his niceness. Sometimes it's just so annoying to be niced at all the time, especially when I'm in the middle of a hissy fit! But then times come along when nice feels really good, such as last week when I was in the hospital puking my drugged out guts up with a kidney stone, and he stayed right there with me for hours until it appeared that I would live to tell the tale (although I'm sure he didn't expect me to tell it this way) and then he went home to take care of our children. Yes, if he were Catholic, he would be heading up the path to sainthood.

And here's another thing about Bret you all should know. He is a rollicking hoot (in a very understated sense of the term). This revelation came to me in an epiphanous moment after I was feeling better. I told him I had read an article in the paper about bald eagles nesting again at Laurel Lake. I asked him if there would be any way we could encourage them to nest in our yard. With nary a bat of an eyelash he answered, "I suppose we could throw some dead chickens out in the yard." I nearly passed another stone, because I could...

At this point, the rest of the June 2003 Doodle fell off the end of the church newsletter with no explanation, so the next month, I wrote the following:

For Those Who Insist on Continuity of Thought

July 2003

Okay, okay, I can take a hint. No one ever accused me of talking too much, but I have been known to ramble on when spilling my brain cells onto paper. And last month I evidently rambled right off the page into cyberspastic oblivion, leaving all you loyal readers scratching your collective heads and muttering, "She's gone and left us hanging by our suspenders just like all those television shows do in the spring when they're desperate to get us back wasting our time again in the fall!"

Never fear! I won't make you wait until October to read the rest of the story. I'm desperate for you to waste your time reading this enriching blather every month of the year! And so, since July is the month of independence, watermelon and fireworks, I hereby grasp my first amendment right to free speech in hand, while spitting the juicy ending of June's Doodle into the furthest reaches of church newsletterdom before (I hope) the computer explodes again.

As I was saying, we need to appreciate the men in our lives. They add more than just annoyances to our existence. My man, Bret, adds laughter to mine. He is a hoot. As we were talking about eagles nesting at Laurel Lake, I asked him if there would be any way we could encourage them to nest in our yard. (We now join the June Doodle already in progress.) With nary a bat of an eyelash he answered, "I suppose we could throw some dead chickens out in the yard." I nearly passed another stone, because I could picture him actually doing that if a desperate need for eagle nesting sites should ever arise!

One last anecdote, and I will hush so that you may dredge up your own joyous thoughts about your own special guys. Bret's hootiness goes so deep he even dreams funny. Here's a dream he had several months ago right before we moved into our new sanctuary: He was sitting before the new sound board with a hound dog beside him. Pastor Tim came up and asked, "Bret, what's the dog doing here?" Bret answered, "Well, I asked Ed (the minister of music) if he had any pointers for me, and he said this was the best he could do!"

I'm not sure what this says about Ed, but it reminds me of why Bret deserves the award for Best Husband I Ever Had. Happy Father's Day! (Belated) And Happy Independence Day!

For Wantonly Weepy Wordsmiths

August 2003

One more time should do it. After taking a two month break from my current obsession with Amy's imminent departure for college, into the hilarity of life with my hubby, I feel a deep need to plunge into the maudlin murkiness of motherhood one last time, before all my past Amy-angst becomes resigned reality at the end of this month. You'll have to get over it, people, and endure one more waaah! from the mom-who-must-snip-snip-before-her-overstretched-apron-strings-strangle-her-and-everyone-around-her.

Tears of Embellishment

My tears splatter
like rain from a mackerel sky,
unexpected,
ludicrous as lop-eared bunnies in mackinaws
squaring off for a grudge match,
unexplainable
as Rush Limbaugh with lockjaw.
They travel curvilinear paths
over cheeks old enough to know better,
yet still too young to store them up
for greater griefs to come.
I wave one last time,
a plaster smile serving as riverbank
to the inevitable flood,
as she, oblivious, skips toward her dorm room,
determined to wring every last drop from life
before it starts wringing her.
I turn away to go home,
memories of rocking horse patrol
my bane and my tonic,
streaky make-up,
the only embellishment
worthy of the day.
God go with you, daughter.
I hope I did my job.

SNIP! SNIP! Off to Asbury she goes with money and dreams given by God. And off I go back to driving a lot more and preparing for another snipping in three short years. Waaaaah! Did you really expect this to be the end of it?

For Spiritual Cooks

September 2003

Here's a recipe for spiritual growth you may not have tried. It's not exactly tasty, but if you follow it, I guarantee something extraordinary will happen.

Early in the morning, combine the following:
One van packed full of teenage possessions and five exhausted people
One trip to the oral surgeon to fix a wisdom tooth extraction wound abscess
Hundreds of tiny baby ticks crawling up a ten-year-old's leg
One construction zone speeding ticket
Several liters of snot packed into three girls' heads

In the afternoon, add with a frenzy:
Four hungry people munching on popcorn while wandering around a gym
One hungry girl with a sore mouth munching on nothing while waiting in lines
As many people as you can grab to unload van and haul teenage life up three flights of stairs
Much furniture shoving and loud banging on bed rails
Miraculous squeezing of two teenage girls' lives into one tiny room
Two big smiles on teenage girls' faces
One mad crawl during a rush hour lightning show to a motel to change clothes

Debra Kuss

In the evening, mix in gently:
A convocation service in a beautiful chapel with hundreds of families from all over the country
A litany releasing your very own young woman into the care of God's servants at Asbury
Tears of joy, awe, and sadness splattering a hymnal
A reminder from the morning's reading in Rick Warren's *The Purpose Driven Life* that life is a test and a trust

Finally, remain calm and allow God's grace to knead this concoction into your soul. Give God the glory for his blessings far beyond all you could ask or think.

For Those Who Have Waited Patiently to Read Something Spiritual in this Space

October 2003

Once again, dear doodleheads (my pet name for those of you who courageously step into the depths of doodledom each month, hoping that perhaps something spiritually worthy of your time will reach out and knock you in the head) I come to you with thoughts all a-boggled. As you may have noticed, I've been swirling in a vortex of apron string snipping for approximately a year. Suddenly, I find myself cut loose and slung out to sea with all manner of disconnected thoughts circling around my rather teensy raft of sanity. Yes, it is time to do some rowing and find out what else has been going on since I disappeared into the whirlpool of mother-angst last September.

First, I was involved in the Beth Moore *Believing God* study in Sunday School. I am happy to report that I am still not over it. God truly does speak and work in our lives on a daily basis—we just need to take the time to notice and be awestruck. Amy would very possibly not be at Asbury if it were not for that study, because we would not have had the courage to believe God for it. We are still learning and believing, especially when the bills somehow manage to get paid and we're not even starving!

Secondly, I am officially old. Not only do I have a child in college, but I have celebrated my silver wedding anniversary. Talk about believing God! Evidently Bret (the Kuss saint) must have learned the secret long ago to seeing beyond the obvious (Debbie, the weirdo) to the possible with God (Debbie, the weirdo that might turn out okay after many years of prayer). Stay tuned to see if the reality ever matches the dream—maybe in another 25 years.

Thirdly, speaking of dreams, Bret's hound dog dream has come true. We are now the proud parents of a four-month-old Bloodhound named Eujane. I'm sure she will be the purveyor of many spiritual insights in the years to come.

Finally, I am now in *The Purpose Driven Life* study in Sunday School. Thus far I have learned what a total bleck I am as a Christian. My purposes need an overhaul! It's a great study, even though it is annoyingly disturbing. Here's one positive thought from it to give me hope: "being confident of this, that he who began a good work in you will carry it on to completion until the day of Christ Jesus" (Philippians 1:6 NIV). Now that's a great promise, especially for old, mind-boggled weirdos!

For God's Works in Progress

November 2003

People, people, PEOPLE!!! I'm so excited! And it has nothing to do with Paul McCartney! Or babies entertaining me with their funny antics all day! Or children going off with bits of my heart and soul dragging in the dirt behind them! Or even my sudden obsession with exclamation points! No, this goes way beyond all that superficial emotion I have so blessed you with over the years. This great excitement goes way, way deep, to the point that it has changed my whole perspective on life, so hey, I figure I might ought to share it with you dear friends who have endured my somewhat warped perspective for way too long.

Last month I mentioned that I was involved in the Sunday School class studying *The Purpose Driven Life* by Rick Warren. At that time, I was rather depressed about my apparent failure as a Christian to live up to all the important purposes God had created me to fulfill. I felt like a big pile of garbage that should be thrown out. (Just so you know, I've always struggled with going over the edge of the pit of doom and wallowing there, so don't avoid the book—it's great.) Anyway, the very next day after writing the October Doodle, I came to chapter 30 which contains the single most mind-blowing statement ever to penetrate this melancholic brain. Rick Warren quotes Ephesians 2:10 (NIV) "For we are God's workmanship, created in Christ Jesus to do good works, which God prepared in advance for us to do," and then he says, "our English word *poem* comes from the Greek word translated *workmanship.*" I've read that verse countless times in various translations, and even though "workmanship" is often translated "masterpiece" I never managed to see myself as that. That word simply didn't resonate with me since I equated masterpiece with visual art for some reason. But now, knowing that the Greek word used there, "poiema" literally translates to "poem," I am beside myself with pure joy! I understand poetry!! I understand that poems don't just splat out on the page fully formed and finished at the moment of inspiration. They can go through all kinds of changes before reaching completion.

People! Talk about a life verse! I'm God's POEM! We're all God's anthology of His greatest works of art! Does this not make you just stomp your feet and yell and carry on like a holy-rollin' Pentecostal (at least in the privacy of your own bathroom—which is where I went as soon as I got up off the floor after reading that)? And what makes this analogy so much more meaningful is knowing that we are works in progress, rough drafts that God is continually tweaking by erasing a word here and there, or adding a whole new stanza, or changing the title, or smoothing out a rough rhythm, until someday we are perfected and published right into heaven! Just because we're not perfect now doesn't mean that we're hopeless. God simply hasn't finished us yet.

And here's another exciting poetic thought. God, as the universal Poet Laureate, is skilled in creating all types of poems, from epic ballads to free verse to haiku to sestinas—different forms to express the same message to different hearts. That means we don't have to waste time wishing we had a different personality. If you're a haiku, God created you to touch people who would rather read a haiku than a ballad. He didn't just accidentally leave out a bunch of words. I could go on and on. But I will practice restraint and say just one more thing: if you aren't going to Sunday School, you should try it. Astounding stuff happens there.

For the Musically Challenged Christmas Frenzied

December 2003

Since my recent enlightenment on my status as God's poem, I'm finding myself thinking in rhyme about the upcoming holy holiday. Unfortunately, I'm not as great a poet as God, so the rhyme's not so hot, but it will do for this Christmas doodle. Last year I was hearing crazy voices in my head (Nellie and Lulu); this year it's bad parodies of Christmas carols. Go figure. We all have our crosses to bear. This, I'm afraid, is one of yours. To the tune of one of my favorite carols—hit it, Choir!

Oh Little Town of Corbin

1.) Oh little town of Corbin
How frenzied the days go by
Before the celebration of
The babe who came to die.
Yet in our hearts we wonder
What all the fuss is about
We shop and cook and decorate
Until we near pass out!

2.) We spend and clean and worry
If what we've done will please
The ones we love most on this earth--
Why don't we hit our knees?
So little thought we give Him
When all our plans we make.
We surely knew He'd be there.
So where's His birthday cake?

3.) Someday, I pray, we'll see Him
The Christ this is all about
We'll fall before His perfect face
With silence and with shout.
We'll see the nail scars driven
Into His hands by us.
We'll see our Christmas gift--Himself--
Real joy without the fuss.

Joyous Christmas!

Blessed New Year!

For the Enlarged and Stretched

January 2004

Now that we are all back from wherever we were over the holidays, it's time for some deep and self-evaluating thought. After all, isn't that the beauty of a new year? While we're sitting around in our enlarged and lethargic holiday bodies, we can make all kinds of resolutions to improve ourselves, set goals, formulate formulas for simplifying our rat race lives, and set schedules for achieving all these noble plans.

Unfortunately, when I sat down to write this (while still full throttle in the pre-holiday frenzy) nary a deep or self-evaluating thought came to me (unless you count the banshee cry of my soul at that time of year: "If everybody would just leave me alone, I could finish this joyful holiday stuff and get some sleep!", but I don't count that because it's too scary). In other words, I had nothing to say worth a doodle.

Perhaps you would think that would make me stop and say, "Hey, maybe I should give everyone a rest this month." But no, I already did that once, and I hate to repeat myself unless it involves mother-angst, stress mismanagement, or Paul McCartney. Instead I went with the old tried and true desperate-for-a-word-from-God method—I prayed for God to give me a verse and something to say about it, then I plopped my Bible down and let it fall open. Already I hear the disdainful chortling out there from those of you who have tried this and ended up with I Chronicles 26:1 (NIV) "The divisions of the gatekeepers: From the Korahites: Meshelemiah son on Kore, one of the sons of Asaph." I'm sure Pastor Tim could preach a while on that subject, but let's be honest—most of us are glad he hasn't.

Anyway, all chortling must cease, because this time my Bible plopped open to a doozy of an appropriate spot—Isaiah 54:2-3 (NIV): "Enlarge the place of your tent, stretch your tent curtains wide, do not hold back; lengthen your stakes. For you will spread out to the right and to the left…" That's the passage our new church building is based on, the scripture that verified the vision to build, given to some of our members over 25 years ago! And guess when we moved into our new sanctuary? Last January! It has been a whole year. Maybe God wants us to take some time this month to remember, praise, and stretch those curtains ever wider. Isn't it exciting that God always has something to say that's worth a doodle?

For the Thoughtishly Challenged

February 2004

The devil is after my brain. Being of the melancholy personality persuasion, I have a hard time staying out of the slough of despond that John Bunyan described in *The Pilgrim's Progress* way back in the 1600's. He said,

> The name of the slough was Despond. And here, therefore, they wallowed for a time, being grievously bedaubed with dirt... It is the descent whither the scum and filth that attends conviction for sin doth continually run, and therefore it was called the Slough of Despond: for still, as the sinner is awakened about his lost condition, there ariseth in his soul many fears, and doubts, and discouraging apprehensions, which all of them get together and settle in this place.

You may ask why a Christian would ever wind up in the scum and filth of sin conviction when all he needs to do is confess to the Lord to be forgiven and cleansed (1 John 1:9). Well, as I was reminded in Sunday School just a few weeks ago, we can be forgiven by God, but continue to wallow in our guilt by listening to the lies we hear in our heads: "You're no good. You'll never get it right. God will never be able to use a goof-up like you. You might as well just call it quits before you mess up any more lives."

Another great writer, John Milton, revealed Satan's ultimate plan of attack for humanity, when in *Paradise Lost* Satan says, "The mind is its own place, and in itself can make a Heaven of Hell, a Hell of Heaven." It's all a mind game, people! Satan knows that better than anyone. He's been playing the game since he had his little talk with Eve back in Eden. We can listen to God or we can listen to the devil. And the listening doesn't stop when we get saved. If Satan fails to make a heaven of hell in our brains so that we refuse to see our need for Christ, he's going to try twice as hard to make a hell of heaven for us so that we become mired in life's messy sloughs of despond that seem to slosh over our road to the Celestial City at regular intervals.

As the greatest writer of all once said to Moses, found in Deuteronomy 30:19–20 (NIV) "…I have set before you life and death, blessings and curses. Now choose life, so that you and your children may live and that you may love the Lord your God, listen to his voice, and hold fast to him. For the Lord is your life. . ."

The next time I feel myself slipping into the muck, I'm grabbing my hearing aid (the Bible) before I go under, and shout with a heavenly holler, "Shut up, Satan! I'm listening to God!"

For the Regressing Progressing Christian

March 2004

Hello fellow pilgrims! March is upon us and I'm suddenly astounded by the fact that my three favorite teeny weeny people are about to become two-year-olds. I cannot believe that I've been a nanny for two whole years already. What a blessing the last couple of years have been as I've cuddled, fed, burped, cleaned, dressed, rocked, coaxed, wiped, carried, chased, read to, played with, and "no-noed" my way through all their phases and moods, without losing sleep at night or worrying about how to pay for them. Nannydom rocks!

And now we stand at the brink of the Tremendous Two's. Thinking about the upcoming milestones causes me to laugh and cringe at the same time (think watching a funny movie while recuperating from abdominal surgery). I'm also noticing some striking similarities between the two-year-old lifestyle and the Christian walk that most of us find ourselves on—The Pilgrim's Regression/Progression:

1. Learning to undress and dress is not so hard. Learning to stay dressed can take a while. (Ephesians 6 talks about putting on the full armor of God to fight off the enemy. I tend to find myself in a state of partial armor often, as my helmet crashes to the ground and my breastplate slips while I'm concentrating on grabbing my shield as I fly out the door.)

2. Singing the ABC song is fun. Learning how to use those letters well takes years. (Learning what the Word says is relatively easy. Applying it to life takes a lifetime.)

3. Hearing Mommy, Daddy or Nanny's words is easy. Obeying is another matter that often involves pain. (Does this even need an illustration?)

4. Learning to use the potty can be a messy business. (I don't want to think about how this relates to the Christian life, but I know I make a lot of messes that need cleaning up.)

There you have it—a look into the next twelve months and the rest of my life all in one package. Happy Birthday, Joshua, Catherine and Christopher!

For Everyone Who Has Ever Lived

April 2004

Easter is upon us once again! I hope you're experiencing it with a fresh sense of gratitude as I am. Since seeing *The Passion of the Christ*, which God made me see even though I didn't want to, I have a whole new perspective on Christ's sacrifice. Throughout the entire movie I heard Isaiah 53:5 (NIV) playing in my head: "But he was pierced for our transgressions, he was crushed for our iniquities; the punishment that brought us peace was upon him, and by his wounds we are healed."

Mel Gibson quoted this verse as one that was instrumental in leading him to recommit his life to God a dozen or so years ago, when he was a rich, famous, miserable mess. Soon after that, the vision for this movie came to him. His personal quest became a personal encounter with Christ for every Christian who sees it. Christ's wounds can no longer remain a fuzzy metaphor once a person sees them for what they were in living color. They offend those who do not understand their mysterious, healing power, but they scream love and mercy to those of us who realize that Christ bore those stripes in our place to heal our miserably messy lives, not just once, but every time we find ourselves enmeshed in a battle against sin or plain old discouragement. Here's a poem (surprise!) I wrote when I was feeling discouraged by the frantic dailyness of life:

Pressing On

I used to focus on the dream
of making my life count.
I'd lead and teach and use my time
to help the world become sublime
with love and peace--no room for crime!
Ideals flowed like a fount.

Then life became a silent scream
of stress to get things done.
Just treading through the thick malaise
of daily chores filled all my days
and fear let dreams slip into haze
and vanish one by one.

I can't keep up this hectic pace.
Relentless in my drive
for pleasure, fortune and success,
I've starved my soul, I must confess,
and now I long for God's caress
while I am still alive.

With new resolve to seek His face
and claim the joy fear stole--
those wasted days I must not clasp,
worm-eaten years beyond my grasp,
beginning now, my buried past--
I'll press on toward the goal!

For Anyone Who Has
Ever Had a Mother

May 2004

Hey, it's May again! And because I have no one performing in a huge, time-and-brain-cell-consuming play or about to fly the warm, safe nesty coop this year, I find myself thinking about something other than my own personal children and my own personal sleep deprivation. This year, my thoughts have turned toward Mother's Day and Memorial Day.

For me, the two have been linked closely together for nineteen years. It was nineteen years ago on Mother's Day that I last saw my mother alive. She was in the final stage of lung cancer, I was 28 years old with a seven-month-old baby, and neither one of us knew how to say goodbye, so we didn't. I left to go back to my home and my job four hours away, thinking I would see her again in a few weeks, but secretly praying I wouldn't. She needed it to be over and so did I. Eight days later, my sister called to say Mama was gone. I've always regretted that I wasn't strong enough to make sure I would be there to see her off, and that we ran out of time before we could enjoy being mothers together.

Three years later my dad died of the same disease. I wasn't with him when he left this earth either, but I was in the same city, seeing my four-year-old and nine-month-old at the other grandparents' house between hospital visits. He was a veteran of World War II, so his coffin was draped in the flag and "Taps" was played at his burial. When I see Memorial Day services replayed on the news, I think of him. Needless to say, May is not the happiest month for me.

And yet, I see how God had "plans to give me hope and a future" (Jeremiah 29:11) years ago. At the age of eleven, I met my future in-laws when they knocked on our door to invite us to church. I went, and not only ended up marrying their best son, but growing to love and respect them as Christian mentors as well as parents. They've been a part of my life now longer than my own parents were! Then there's my sister. She is sixteen years older than I and was married when I was two. We never had much of a relationship until Mama died. Now I'm closer to her than I ever was to my mom. And my girls have an aunt and uncle who are as close to another set of grandparents as they could ever wish for.

Honor your parents while they're still around, and if they're already gone, remember them often and be on the lookout for those whom God sends your way to fill the empty spaces. He is good—all the time.

For the Unconformed Confirmed

Ahoy, fellow adventurers! I greet you from the Sea of Frenzquility. At this moment I am sitting at Galaxy Bowling in Richmond watching the Confirmation class of 2004 wreak havoc upon noisy wooden pins with heavy glow-in-the-dark balls. Why am I not also indulging in the hilarity of wreakdom, you may ask? I will answer you with a statement of deep profundity uttered by our wise and wacky pastor in one of this weekend's confirmation sessions. He said, "All God wants from you is to be yourself, because He created you the way you are. If you're a rabbit, don't join the swim team."

Great gobs of godly goodness! Oh, that I had heard that when I was eleven or twelve! I could have avoided years of frustration and misery trying to be what other people wanted me to be, while doing things I thought I should be doing for God. I was doing my best to live up to the first part of Romans 12: 2 (NIV), "Do not conform any longer to the pattern of this world, but be transformed by the renewing of your mind." Silly deluded wabbit! I somehow missed getting the second part of the verse, "Then you will be able to test and approve what God's will is—his good, pleasing and perfect will." I thought I was doing His will by saying yes to everything anyone asked of me, because I figured God must have led them to ask me. Sometimes that turned out to be true, but many times I found myself hopping frantically around the bottom of a pool looking for a ladder to climb out.

Then I went one better by *volunteering* to do all manner of things because the need was there. My waterlogged brain took on a twisted Kentucky lottery jingle mindset— "Somebody has to do it. Might as well be me!" And that was after a good friend of mine shared these words of wisdom with me—"The need is not the call, Debbie." This poor drenched rabbit spent so much time and energy trying to keep from drowning in the pool, she was too exhausted to hop around in her natural God-created habitat. And she kept wishing she could swim better!

So that takes us back to your oh, so innocent question of why I'm not bowling instead of writing this. God made me an odd, non-swimming, non-bowling, non-chitchatting, nervous nose-twitching rabbit who skitters from social activities to hide in the underbrush to write poetry, doodles, and other such business. I'm through with swimming! Thanks Tim, for confirming me as a rabbit. Let's pray that our newest church members will quickly find their own God-given habitat in which to serve Him.

For Doodleheads

July 2004

Hello from the humid depths of summer, fellow doodleheads! After our exhilarating week of VBS, I find myself totally brain dead. That means that you, my faithful readers, are in for a dose of poetry ripped from the pages of my pre-VBS brain.

Like all great writers and artists who have "periods" when certain themes or styles dominate their work (the Lucy period, the Blue period, the Psycho period, the Way-Too-Deep period), we not-so-great writers and artists experience our own unique periods as well. I, for instance, seem to be in my Bloodhound period. In the last six months I have written three poems with references to bloodhounds. This could be attributed to some deep-seated poetic metaphor suddenly bursting forth with creative vengeance in my soul, but more likely, it is the slobbering, crying bloodhound pup bursting into my face every morning at breakfast that has brought this on. Whatever the case, here's some drool-induced poetry for you to contemplate on your summer vacation. (Please do not hold me responsible for any dreams you may experience if you read this before a nap. Also, do not ask me what it means. It's way too deep.)

The Hunt

The forest looms before me deep and still
So full of life and terror while I wait.
And then the chase is on against my will.
The hounds come baying, charging through the gate
    like country Pentecostals
    praising God
    joyfully off key
    on local cable access.
The Hunter, smiling, steps out from the gloom,
His weapon loaded with his own spilled blood.
He shoots and I fall prostrate at his feet.
The forest looms before me deep and still.

For Everyone Who Needs
a Smack in the Head

August 2004

Does anybody out there need a smack in the head? I do. God is trying to tell me something and so far He's being very nice about it. He just keeps bringing it up over and over and over. Evidently, I'm not getting it, or He would move on to a different topic, don't you think?

First we plowed through Beth Moore's *Believing God* study in Sunday School a year and a half ago. That was great and I'm still muttering those five pledge of faith statements to myself, especially when our monthly Asbury College payment comes in the mail. Then last fall we whizzed through Rick Warren's *The Purpose Driven Life*, where I learned that I am God's poem, a thought that still makes me break into a joyous rendition of "Oh, Happy Day!" whenever it crosses my mind. Next came Beth Moore's fruit of the Spirit study, *Living Beyond Yourself* this spring, and Pastor Tim's fruit of the Spirit series in church, and his rabbit on the swim team Confirmation class story, and now we're back into *The Purpose Driven Life* in a summer Sunday School class! Does this sound to you like God is trying to tell me something? Or am I just imagining that all of this connects into one big lesson that I need to learn?

"Well," you may ask, "what exactly is it that you think God is trying to teach you, doodlebrain?" Thank you for asking! I think it may be something such as I need to believe that He created me just the way He wanted me, in order for me to live my life fulfilling the purposes He has for me, while I become more like Jesus through His Holy Spirit's indwelling, which will cause me to exude the fruit of the Spirit for all to see, so others are drawn to Him!" Very simple, but not so easy to do consistently.

I'm sure most of us are on the same journey through the jungle of life, trying to stay on God's path for us, but periodically getting off into the thorns of everyday demands, or the swamp of self-disgust, or some annoying person starts plucking our fruit right off the vine, or the devouring lion himself distracts us just as we're working on a really good purpose, or some well-meaning person convinces us to swim in our rabbit fur coat. It can be downright trying to the soul!

And that reminds me of Rick Warren's statement that "Life is a test and a trust." And Beth Moore's battle cry, "I'm Believing God!" And Tim's point that the fruit of the Spirit has to be cultivated (with some good old stinky manure, I presume). And my personal doodlebrain thought, "Poetic rabbits look stupid when wet!"

Maybe I am getting it, bit by bit. But please, if you see me running around looking depressed, or wet, or dense—just smack me in the head! And I'll do the same for you. According to Purpose #2, that's called accountability.

For Potential Guest Columnists

September 2004

Welcome back to the dense forest of Friedbraindom! Since last we met, things have not improved much on the brain front, due to school starting again. One would think something like that would infuse one with deep and educated thoughts. Perhaps it does do that for one, but not for me. School just makes me denser than whatever you can think of that is dense. Getting up way too early, driving back and forth about town, freaking out about group homework assignments, coordinating shower and internet schedules, and trying to work in a few personal thoughts now and then wears me out. At this point, I'm on the lookout for a few brave guest columnists. So far, the following have come to mind:

Eujane, the bloodhound, would make a great guest columnist. She has so much more to say than I do. Her soulful face reeks empathy for all the foibles of mankind. I'm teaching her French so maybe she can intercede between us and France, because I'd really like to go back to Paris someday and not feel guilty about it. Arrrarrrarrrooooooey means "take me for a walk along the Seine, or I'll slobber on your neck."

Erin, the middle daughter, for sure could take a turn at this profoundly responsible position. She would love to tell you about her band, *Fergen*, and her brilliant Irish friend, *Shule*, and her closet full of *movie stars,* and her famous *ribbon game* that is sweeping certain important parts of the nation, and she would also love to give you a total *fashion makeover*. Just ask her!

P.B., the healthy singing woman, may also like to be a guest columnist someday. She suggested that I might want to write a Doodle about funeral songs. This is an excellent idea, since two groups of us were discussing the songs we want to hear at our funerals while we were bonding at a Beth Moore conference. Bret, the husband, never likes it when I remind him and the girls about the songs I want at my funeral--Let It Be, The Long and Winding Road, Yesterday, Amazing Grace, One Day and others to be added as the mood strikes (me, not them). But ha! Now I know I'm not the only one who likes to plan ahead for such important events. Maybe it's a woman thing.

Carly, Amy, and Bret, the other Kuss people, do not want to be guest columnists. They would rather you not know what they are thinking beneath their deceptively quiet exteriors. In other words, they are chicken. Maybe after this, they will step forward and save you nice people from another one of these completely irrelevant ravings.

And now that you know how truly desperate I am, perhaps *you* would like to spill your spiritual guts in my stead sometime. Many people would thank you, I'm sure. Get some sleep and have a great September!

For the Not So Intensely Clean

October 2004

Here we are again in that most beautiful of seasons—Fall. And in order to do my part in keeping this season beautiful I have been engaging in the highly amusing extreme sport of Fall Cleaning. This is not a sport for the timid or weak. Fall Cleaning demands tremendous brawny strength, aggressive hormonal adrenaline, and a fair amount of in-laws-on-the-way motivation. When these three collide, spider castles and dust bunny villages have no hope of survival. Frenzied Female will conquer! While I've been in this mode, lamenting the futility of my super scrubbing in the face of relentless dirt arsenals that never run out of ammunition, God has brought to mind a couple of parallels between housework and Hiswork.

Although we at the Kuss home own several trash receptacles, I seem to be the only one who knows where they are. That means little piles of paper and junk stack up in various places around the house. And I, being the patiently annoyed mother, ignore them for months and sometimes years, hoping that the people responsible for these piles will do something about them. Eventually my hormones explode into a holy rage and I gather up all the ignored crud piles that have become well established homes to little crawly creatures and deposit them in the aforementioned receptacles. The very next day, all the other Kusses suddenly begin thrashing about looking for desperately needed items that they left on the couch or in a corner of the kitchen or draped over the rocking chair back in the last century. And of course, Frenzied Female is to blame for all their troubles. Well, let me tell you, Frenzied Female becomes a little testy when that happens! And I imagine God is not too happy with me when I ignore things in my life that He has given me to do, or don't take care of messes that I need to take care of, and then I come whining to Him when He finally makes a move to clean house. It's a lot less painful for both of us when I do my own house cleaning. Thankfully, God is much more merciful than Frenzied Female.

No matter how hard I try, I cannot eliminate the filth that infiltrates my house. All I can do is try to keep it from becoming a major biohazard. Spiritually, I cannot make sin go away completely. In fact, at those times when I think I've finally clunked my sinful self in the head with a death blow, Satan springs up and laughs in my face as I turn around and trip over another sin heap. Every day, I have to get out the dust rag of confession and the can of Holy Spirit polish and get to working. If I don't keep on top of things, I'll end up with a soul that's a spiritual health risk.

Remember, when your own personal Frenzied Female goes on dirt patrol like a screaming banshee, either get out of the way and pray for mercy, or pick up a broom and help her on her noble crusade against filth! These biannual freak outs will not be going away anytime soon. Happy Fall to y'all!

For Rerun Fans

December 2004

Christmas is upon us once again and I find myself wondering what I could possibly write about that I haven't already spewed forth in the last four years. In 2000, I shared how Christmas changed for me the year my older brother was in Vietnam instead of at home with our family. (Three years ago he became a Methodist pastor of two rural churches and can barely find the time to celebrate a family Christmas—but nobody minds since he has finally found God's calling for his life.) In 2001, in a fit of frenzy, I tried to cancel Christmas, but instead, decided to cancel one or two of the frenzy-causing chores I always make for myself. In 2002, the Cerebralspasm sisters living in my brain, Nellie and Lulu, gave you a scary peek inside my holiday thought processes. (I believed they had moved off into some other hapless soul's mind, until I heard Lulu screaming this morning that if we go to Kansas City for the week before Christmas, that leaves only three weeks after Thanksgiving to get everything finished. At this, Nellie, the sensible, muttered, "Oh, oh, oh!" and collapsed heavily upon my brain tissue, causing an Excedrin headache even Excedrin could not touch.)

That leads me to last year's Doodle, when a Christmas carol parodying mood took over my life for a few weeks, and I wrote a little ditty that several people seemed to like. Since the message is something I sorely need to hear again, now that the crazy brain sisters are back, I thought maybe you wouldn't mind hearing it again, also.

TIME WARP TIME WARP TIME WARP TIME WARP

BUT WAIT!!! Let us sproing into the future. The year is 2017 and I am working on making my collection of church newsletter Doodles into a book. I can't expect my present-day readers to endure a rerun just a few pages after the original writing, even though a whole year had passed between Christmas Doodles for the original readers. That would be such a numbing disappointment to those of you reading right this minute! Hmmm. I must think of something seasonally appropriate right now, which is thirteen years later.

Perhaps I should simply let you in on the secret of life that I have finally learned (some days it's clearer than others) in the last thirteen years. Get ready. This is HUGE! Here's the secret: LIFE GOES ON, and it happens one day at a time. Thirteen years after writing my original December 2004 Doodle, I am again preparing for the holiday season, but it's as different as it is the same in 2017. My dearly beloved and I have been empty nesters for over two years. All three daughters are out living their own lives. The oldest has been married for ten years and has three children (we were anticipating the arrival of the third soon after the holidays just last year). The other two daughters are living the adventures of single women right now. We still have a bloodhound, but not the same one. Eujane passed away in 2015, as well as my sister and her husband. Life is certainly different than it was in 2004, but it is much the same as well. The seasons seem to whirl by even more quickly than when our house was full of teenage girl chaos.

Here's my new 2004 Christmas message to you, coming straight from the future: *Enjoy life as it is right now. Keep your eyes open for God moments every day. Love your family while you have them. Stay open to whatever new adventures are just around the bend. Be the poem God created you to be! And always have a Merry Christmas!*

For the Newly Challenged, or the Oldly Challenged in a New Way, or the Constantly Challenged in Every Way—Take Your Pick

January 2005

Happy New Year people! I'm going to project myself into the future a bit (which isn't hard for me since that's where my mind seems to live most of the time anyway) because at this very moment, Christmas has not actually happened yet. In fact, school is not even out, we (meaning the Kusses) have not made the annual Christmas pilgrimage across the frozen plains to our personal Mecca (Kansas City) and we (meaning Doodledoo Debbie) are still in the pre-joyful, not-yet-able-to-relax-and-experience-the-true- meaning-of-Christmas mode. The writing of the January Doodle is my last major assignment before joy hits me in the head with a Hallelujah Chorus. Let's make this snappy, then!

WWWWAAAARRRRPPPPP! Here I am three weeks into the future. It's a happy place. Not much going on. Just the usual calm school mornings, peaceful days with the quiet little triplets, relaxing evenings in front of the fire with my loving family and docile, sweet smelling dog. Aaaahhh. ***BOOM! CRASH! SPROING! MAY DAY! MAY DAY! BRAIN ALERT! SPLAT! OUCH!***

Ooops, I forgot. When projecting oneself into the future, reality sometimes takes a while to catch up with fantasy. It looks like the same old world around here. Hectic days, noisy (yes, the Kusses do make noise in the privacy of their own home) and busy, sometimes smelly evenings, depending on what Eujane, the bloodhound, has been into during the day. And we don't actually have a fire, unless you count the occasional eruptions on the stove. But wait! I see something different. A new thing has invaded the atmosphere! It's Debbie trying desperately (of course) to see the world through the faith eyes of a child instead of the fading fast eyes of a middle-aged neurotic woman.

This is really, totally weird. Apparently, Debbie experienced an epiphany during the Christmas season while conversing with the triplets about Santa Claus and baby Jesus. While reading storybooks and looking at pictures, suddenly she was transported back a few years when her girls were itty bitty and believed anything she told them. The wonder of a child with completely doubtless faith is a priceless gift to be treasured in our hearts forever—and then emulated. Jesus said in Matthew 18:3 (NIV) "I tell you the truth, unless you change and become like little children, you will never enter the kingdom of heaven." Our faith needs to be as pure as a child's—faith that believes whatever God says, and then lives in expectation of the fulfillment.

Hey! This must be Debbie's New Year's resolution. Hot Smelly Doggie! This time warp thing comes in handy. Now I don't have to ponder and gnash my teeth about what to resolve for 2005. It's not even Christmas and I'm ahead of the game for next year. Let the *expectation* and *joy* begin!

For Birthday Inspired Poetry Lovers—and Others

February 2005

With all the Purpose Driven emphasis this month at church, I nearly decided to make my column more purposeful just to be helpful. But, no! I find myself deep into another-birthday-come-and-gone-angst as I realize that I can no longer celebrate Mardi Gras (Fat Tuesday) with any joy, because I celebrate Fat Everyday with such abandon all year long. And although I love my bloodhound, Eujane, I'm suddenly struck by the fact that she and I really are beginning to look similar and it does not make me happy. (Why didn't we decide on a sleek, smooth Greyhound or a cute little Poodle when we chose a new dog? I could have taken up racing or gotten a curly perm in my spare time instead of joining the wrinkle club.) One good thing about growing older, for me at least, is the profound poetry fodder it produces in my soul. So hold on to your hair, people, and join me in a fond salute to growing older and sparklier! Someday, I'm sure, even this season in life will seem like the good old days.

The Road to Gold

Toenail fungus and out of control chin hair--
the clickety clack of the Golden Years Express
bears down upon me.
Once my biggest problems--
split-ends, homework, and immature bullies
morphed into college term papers
and graduating into marriage.
More adult dilemmas followed--
avoiding early morning wrecks while singing
"She Works Hard for the Money"
and inventing cheap concoctions for supper.
In my twenties I thought I knew stress...
But then along came children—
adorable, lovable, pooping, puking, screaming,
irrational, expensive, piano-practicing children!
I nearly went out of my mind.
But instead my mind went out of me.
Huge, gaping holes exist where brain cells thrived,
brain cells that exploded out my ears
and stuck to my teenagers' heads
like vinyl to hot skin.
And there they dangle, just out of reach,
of no use to me, as their new hosts smirk.
With the last vestiges of clear thought left
I laugh loud and long.
They think I'm a crazy old coot
but I'm really a disco queen
heading for the golden light in the tunnel of love.

For God's Purposeful Poems

March 2005

Hello all you purpose driven people out there! I've left my old-age fest and I'm ready to move on to more purposeful, happy thoughts. As you may remember (or not) I shared the best part of *The Purpose Driven Life* book with you over a year ago when I first went through the study. By now you should have reached it in your reading and I hope you're still dancing with joy over the (holy goose bumps!) idea that you are God's poem—a masterpiece in progress no matter how you may feel about your ability to live up to all those purposes God has for you. Like any poet, He chose to write your life in the form that would convey His message to the specific audience He wants to reach through you. He's busy editing and rewriting parts of your life to make you the image of Himself that will impact your world the most. If you ever struggle with your self-worth the way I do, this should turn you into a hallelujah shouting joy freak at least once a day. And surprise! A poem has come forth from my freakish soul in celebration, which I feel compelled to share. God made me this way. I can't help it.

I am God's Poem

Ephesians 2:10a (NIV) "For we are God's workmanship, (poem) created in Christ Jesus to do good works..."

I am God's poem, the work of His hands,
Inspired by love and the need to be known,
Invested with character much like His own,
Conceived in His mind before life began.
        I am God's poem!

I am God's poem, a work in progress.
No stanza of life ever based on a whim,
But perfectly pointing the reader to Him,
While at the same time, teaching me how to bless.
        I am God's poem!

I am God's poem, a work he ordained
To be what I am, the song of his heart,
With odd little verses and rhythms apart,
That lures others in to sing His refrain.
        I am God's poem!

For Three-Year-Old Christians

April and May 2005

Howdy purposeful poems! I hope this finds you enjoying your unique form and meter in God's purpose-fulfilling poetry journal. (Obviously I haven't gotten over that whole "I am God's poem" thing yet, and I hope I never do.) Even so, I must move on to other topics or you, my beloved readers, will get sick of me, and one of my purposes will come to a desperately forlorn end. Instead, let's talk about what we would have talked about last month had I not been so purpose-minded—my nannied triplets' third birthday, of course! Just like when they turned two last year, I have been struck, not by a block whizzing past my ear, but by a few weird parallels between three-year-olds and my own Christian walk. Perhaps you will be able to relate as well:

1. Three-year-olds like to talk, but they don't always listen well. I'm experiencing déjà vu a lot these days. The triplets chatter, chatter, chatter about anything, everything, and nothing all at once. When each of my girls reached this stage (which seemed to last well into middle school) I thought I would go stark raving mad, especially when one would ask a question such as "Whatcha eating, Mommy" and I would answer, "An apple" and she would reply, "Whatcha eating, Mommy?" and I would answer "An apple." After about the fifth time on this broken record I would grab her precious little face with my loving hands, look her directly

in her sweet little eyes and say, "AN APPLE!" and she would respond with "Oh!" Then we would move on to the next question—"Why?" Does any of this sound at all similar to conversations you've had with God, or am I the only one who jabbers at Him for hours on end and forgets to listen for His response? And then I ask, "Why?" I've felt His loving hands on my face a few times when He's gotten tired of repeating Himself. Thankfully He has more patience than I do.

2. Three-year-olds often have toilet troubles. Either they want to visit every toilet in town just to compare doors, paper rolls, flushing capabilities, and disgusting disease populations, or they don't want to visit any at all—ever! Whichever way grabs them at the moment causes Mommy (and sometimes Daddy). . .

This is where the rest of the April Doodle suddenly disappeared, so in May I began with: As I was saying when my brilliant three-year-old to spiritual life analogy disappeared off the page into newsletter oblivion last month, I find that I must resemble a preschooler to God at times. These astounding examples that clearly cannot be allowed to never see the light of day, no matter how many times I may have to repeat myself, which I hope will never happen again, *shall continue in this book midstream, since you can easily go back and catch the rhythm of the preceding paragraph. . .*

great distress leading to the use of that ancient parental mantra, "Just do it, for crying out loud! As for a spiritual parallel, all I can say is I have often come out of one toilet, straight into another one simply to experience some variety in my bad habits.

3. Three-year-olds want to do everything themselves, unless, of course, that would be convenient for the parents, then they don't. Hmmm. You may think spiritually on your own about this one—unless you don't want to. Feel free to be three if you must!

For Tired Inspiration Seekers

June 2005

Holy Giacomoly, dear readers! (I just loved that headline from the Lexington Herald Leader after Giacomo won the Derby, so I have adopted it as the latest in a long line of happy, holy exclamations I will use when inspired by the right circumstance.) And if another school year coming to a glorious end is not the perfect, happy, holy circumstance, then senility has blossomed fully in my otherwise arid mind.

Or let me put it this way, for those of you who need everything spelled out in a succinct and unadorned style—Yahoo! It's summer! The maddening rush of school mornings and evenings has taken a hiatus for a few weeks, so we can hunker down amid the firefly twinkles and mosquito spray to refuel ourselves to start all over again in August. Lucky for you, I have taken it upon myself to share a few yummy Dove chocolatish inspirational thoughts for you to cut out and apply to your life when the next busy, stressful time comes your way. (Do I hear the shrieking of VBS workers in my ears?)

HINT: If you wrap these musings around rice cake tidbits instead of chocolates, you'll have a low fat, low taste treat that won't tempt you to keep eating until you find that one truly profound inspirational thought, which probably isn't in the following list:

IF I CAN JUST GET THROUGH THIS WEEK, I CAN GO ON TO THE NEXT ONE.

WHEN I GET SO TIRED I CAN'T SEE STRAIGHT, I'LL START LEANING.

WHEN I'M TIRED OF RUNNING HITHER AND YON, I'LL TRY RUNNING THIS WAY AND THAT.

WHEN LIFE HANDS ME LEMONS, I'LL PUCKER UP AND PRAY FOR SUGAR.

IF I NEED A TRULY INSPIRATIONAL THOUGHT, I'LL STICK TO THE BIBLE.

Have a joyful June, you crazy people!

For Sojourners

July 2005

Hello fellow sojourners! Now that we are smack in the middle of summer vacation season, I feel a need to write a little travelogue. There's just one problem—I haven't been anywhere yet. The sad fact is the Kusses hardly ever go anywhere (other than the Gateway to the Great Plains, Kansas City, which isn't exactly a beach, mountain, or Disney World.) This year, however, we may actually take off for parts unknown, if we can just decide between all the unknown parts. So, as usual, I am stressing out over something that should be enjoyable.

Here's the spiritual lesson I am trying to learn from this most current of my brain tizzies: "Do not worry about tomorrow, for tomorrow will worry about itself. Each day has enough trouble of its own." (Matthew 6:34 NIV). That's downright brilliant. All I need to do today is trouble myself about where to go a few weeks of tomorrows from now. Yahoo! Problem solved.

And if we decide to save ourselves the bother and stay home, I have the solution for that tomorrow as well, thanks in part to my soul sister Emily Dickinson who wrote:

Debra Kuss

> *There is no Frigate like a Book*
> *To take us Lands away*
> *Nor any Coursers like a Page*
> *Of Prancing Poetry—*

Whether you're staying or going this summer, relax as much as you can, trust God with the details, and read at least one good book!

For the Sentimental

August 2005

I'm feeling sentimental this month. Maybe it's because my baby girl has just tossed her entire childhood (as well as some of her sisters') out the door, in favor of a cooler, older, more "with it" look for her bedroom. No more Barbies, no more dress up clothes, no more Polly Pocket villages! Or maybe I just miss the good old days when summers seemed to last forever—at least until the end of August. I was ready for school to start again back then. Does anyone want to go back to the 60's with me? Too bad if you don't, because here we go!

Sweatimentality

Shimmering summers sparkled with sweat
   when we were young.
Swinging up a breeze, playing tag and dodge ball,
   we gulped icy lemonade, shirts hiked up,
   glistening in front of the box fan.
Scorching our toes, we danced barefoot ballet
   down the driveway to get the mail.
Sprawling on basement floors, we played marbles
   reveling in cold concrete on sun-baked skin.
Slurping popsicles, we counted train cars
   rumbling past every day at noon,
orange and purple puddles forming at our feet.

Squealing with wickedness, we molded
glow-in-the-dark bracelets from firefly twinkles.
Shushing our giggles, we camped out
on the living room floor where the window fan
sucked damp July air over our soap-scented bodies.
Now summers shimmer outside
air-conditioned windows
lost in relief.

If you haven't done so already, swing, scorch, sprawl, slurp, squeal,
and shush while there are still a few days remaining. God bless us all.

For Quietly Insane Parents

September 2005

Hello from the land of School's-Back-in-Session-So-Let's-Just-Smack-Ourselves-Into-Perpetual-Exhaustion-And-Get-It-Over-With! I know there are those of you out there who are thinking, "What is wrong with this loony bird? School's a wonderful place for our dear children to spend a few hours enriching their intellects and not wreaking havoc at home!" Yes, that is completely true, but the older those beloved offspring get, the more school becomes one long marathon of events that saps the already trickling fountain of youth right out of us parents. That's why, I think, God gives us infants through preschoolers first, so that by the time the teen years arrive, we are already insane, thereby making our inevitable brain death virtually painless. In honor of all of us crazy parents (I really, really hope I'm not the only one) I present this ode with much gratitude to the Lord for putting up with me:

<u>To Should Or Not To Should</u>

I should be deeper than I am.
I should be profound.
I should write of Himalayan Sherpas,
Andy Warhol and cheese fondue.
I should bleed purple pigment
and languish on mildewed hammocks.
I should weep in ancient tribal song

and laugh over coddled milk.
I should raise monuments to dead writers
and take a monkey to shop at Saks.
I should insist on entering an asylum
then escape by trampoline.
I should shout hallelujahs on a runaway train
driven by the Pope and Whoopi Goldberg.
I should be freakishly famous!
Instead I'm deep into laundry and mealtime magic.
I bleed yellow crayon
and fall over at bedtime.
I scream in the shower
and laugh caffeine out my nose.
I build Lego towers
and take monkeys to lunch at McDonald's.
I invented the trampoline asylum club.
I praise God at the end of every day
with a child who thinks I'm the queen.
I'm a mom,
no shoulds about it.

For Hurricane Survivors
and their Friends

October 2005

While growing up in the Midwest, I don't remember ever paying much attention to hurricane reports. Back then there were no 24-hour news and weather channels to keep us informed about what was happening outside our own local area. In Missouri, tornadoes were the big climactic events, and they came on so fast there was very little warning. We just went to the basement when the sky turned green.

That's why when Bret, baby Amy, and I moved to Hattiesburg, Mississippi in August 1985, I was shocked and scared spitless by the hurricane watches and warnings we were under as a new named storm headed up the Gulf each week for the first six weeks we lived there. At first, I couldn't understand why we were being told to stock up on non-perishable food, fill our bathtubs with water, keep plenty of flashlights, candles, batteries, matches, and a portable radio handy, secure outdoor furniture, and be ready to leave low-lying areas. Didn't hurricanes happen on the coast? We were 80 miles north of Gulfport. What could happen in Hattiesburg?

Then we started hearing Hurricane Camille stories—how Hattiesburg had been without power for weeks after she came through in 1969. Flooding and wind had wreaked havoc and people held neighborhood barbecues to keep everyone fed. On the coast, people who lived through the storm, survived by hacking their way through walls and ceilings to escape the storm surge (something I had never heard of before.) Now Katrina has come and made all those Camille stories pale in comparison.

During the four years we lived in Hattiesburg, we made many trips to Gulfport, Biloxi and New Orleans. We enjoyed King cake parties during Mardi Gras, ate red beans and rice, learned to say "Hey!" with six syllables instead of "Hi!" with one, and became the recipients, as well as givers, of many little "happies." We loved our church and all the many loving people who welcomed us "Yankees" into their hearts. Even so, we missed hills, colorful autumns, and snow. We did not like eight month long sweltering summers, roaches the size of small dogs, or fire ants. We moved to Corbin 16 years ago and found some more of God's people here.

I've always loved Psalm 121 which begins, "I lift up my eyes to the hills—where does my help come from? My help comes from the Lord, the Maker of heaven and earth" (NIV). We have some God-beloved folks looking to our hills for help right now. Let's love them in the name of the Maker of heaven and earth as they leave their devastated homes to stay with us in our church for a while.

For Those Who Can Stand
Another Poem

November 2005

Hello people! Here we are in the midst of my most favorite of seasons, Autumn, once again. I love the colors in the leaves, the misty, moisty mornings, and the refreshing briskness in the air. This is the season when God speaks to me in nudges and whispers, telling me to look out over the rolling hills and just "be" for a while, before the season of relentless "doing" takes over my life.

This year God is working on me in the areas of abiding in Him (through *The Secrets of the Vine* by Bruce Wilkinson), sewing and reaping a harvest of spiritual prosperity (through Beth Moore's simulcast conference), and trusting Him with, rather than obsessing over, the unknown details of my daughters' futures (through much emotional turmoil surrounding another upcoming high school graduation.) With all these thoughts fluttering around, gently battering my spiritual brain cells into godly mush, I find myself without even a random thought of weirdness to share with you. These things take time to congeal. Therefore, until the gel wiggles in the bowl, or some other messy metaphor flies forth from the inner depths of profundity, you will have to endure yet another poem, a sonnet written on the road while riding through our Appalachian hills with the triplet family.

Seduction

I hear the whispering voices of the past
Arising on the mist at break of day,
Retelling legends with a storied cast
Of Boone and Crockett, Lincoln, Henry Clay.
Melungeons and the Cherokee replay
Their histories within this mountain land,
A verdant Berber carpet on display
For all to see the work of God's own hand.
I do not know when first I heard this band
Of pioneering kindred spirits speak,
Seducing me with mountain song so grand
I fell in love with every rounded peak.
My soul though foreign born forever thrills
Each time I gaze upon Kentucky hills.

For Christmas Ponderers

December 2005

It has often been said that Christmas is all about children, meaning that we as adults should strive to make sure children everywhere receive their hearts' desires at least once a year. There's nothing wrong with wanting to make Christmas special, but in America this sentiment usually translates into overindulging our own children, while giving donations to various charities that take care of the less privileged among us.

This year God has reminded me once again that Christmas is all about children, but not because of what we need to give them. Christmas is about children because of what they give us, an example of how true faith is lived out. Children enjoy a natural gift for faith. They believe whatever they are taught, whether good or bad. If they are told God is love and He takes care of us, they believe, finding reasons to rejoice no matter what.

I rediscovered this truth as I organized our filing system at home this week. While looking through our Compassion International file, I reread letters from all the children we've sponsored over the years. One thanked us for the Christmas money which enabled her family to have meat for Christmas dinner. Another girl from Rwanda wrote, "Though I do not have a parent, I have God who protects me. I am pleased with the gifts you sent me and I could buy animals for rearing though we had no chance of keeping them by the evil doers stealing them." A year later she was killed in the Rwandan civil war.

Wana from Haiti bought a goat with her Christmas money one year. That summer the goat died in a drought and Wana contracted malaria. Recently she wrote that she was not doing so well due to the hurricane that had damaged much of her country. And yet in every letter, she greets me "in Jesus' name who accepted to die on the Calvary wood so that we have eternal life."

Suzana from Tanzania's mother died recently, but she reminded me, "I continue to pray for you so that God will bless you more." Finally, there's Andres from Columbia, who was sponsored at first by our church's VBS offering. He continues to rejoice that he can attend school at the Compassion project and he amuses me with comments such as, "my hare and I are very affectionate."

Bret asked me the other day why we have so many Compassion children. Maybe I just need to see God through their eyes of simple faith and trust.

I wish you all a faith-filled Christmas!

For the Anticipating Masses

January 2006

Happy New Year once again already! Great holy eons of time, it is 2006! Excuse me one moment, please. AAAARRRRGGGHHHHHHH! YIKESTERS! YOWZZZZAAAAA! EEEKKKSSSKKKAAABOB! This is the year I turn 49! This is the year Erin graduates from high school! This is the year Carly turns 13! This is the year the triplets turn 4! This is the year when who knows what else will happen! This is the year when Jesus may return!! Did you ever really think you would see this year? I mean, really, did you? I didn't. When I was a teenager, just learning about the Second Coming, I was sure Jesus would be swooping out of the sky at any instant to take all of us believers out of this crazy world to start our new life as co-heirs with Him on a brand-spanking new earth. I never, ever expected to see my 30th birthday (that was sooooo old!) much less my 49th. I didn't think society could get any weirder or more warped than it was in the '70's. And yet, here I am raising my own teenagers in a much crazier world than the one I grew up in (although the current fashion styles seem strangely familiar) and we're still waiting for the rapture. What's the deal with that?

I guess it's all about grace. Whereas I think God should be sick and tired of all the world's evil and flagrant rebellion against Him and get on with putting it to a stop, He sees each person as His beloved child whom He desperately longs to see turn to Him in repentance and faith. He continues to wait patiently, offering forgiveness and new life here on this planet, not only to those of us who have known Him for years, but also to the millions who have never heard of Him or who have flat out rejected Him thus far. If it weren't for God's grace, none of us would be here at all. He would have said phooey on us long ago. But instead, "The Lord is not slow in keeping his promise, as some understand slowness. He is patient with you, not wanting anyone to perish, but everyone to come to repentance" (2 Peter 3:9 NIV).

That's why for 2006, I resolve to spread more grace around. If God can practice patient grace with the masses of sinful humanity for thousands of years, surely God-in-me can do it for someone somewhere at least once a day. If you see me being mean or crabby this year, smack me upside the head and say, "Jesus is coming, Debbie. You better be showing some grace."

For the Holey Minded

February 2006

Holey, holey, holey! My brain is so holey I've lost my mind. It has been leaking out ever so slowly for quite some time now, but lately my brain has become a sieve filtering out all my own personal thoughts, appointments, plans, and dreams, while piling up with everyone else's stuff. My mind is now the official personal receptacle for all the daily mundane business no one else cares to mess with, plus the inevitable crises that come swirling up out of the murky cauldron of life.

Need something urgently for school? Just let me know, but be sure to tell me as I walk in the door from a marathon shopping trip to Walmart, Kroger, Lowe's and Big Lots. That's when I'm most likely to feel your pain deeply with a heart rending howl. Got a major clothing emergency? Pour it all out to me at midnight as I lay out my fifteen-year-old dress to wear to church the next day. My heart will be wrung with angst over your fashionless life as I search for my '70's shoes that will give your outfit that authentically retro look. Need a ride here, there and everywhere for you and six of your closest-in-heart but farthest-flung-around-town friends? Don't stress—what else could I possibly have to do on a Saturday afternoon? My brain and the body loosely connected to it are at your disposal 24 hours a day until the whole thing implodes with a sizzling fizzle. Then you are on your own.

I feel better now. Perhaps in a few years, when all this is behind me and the house is as empty as my used up holey brain, I can work on rebuilding my mind into a holy receptacle of God's thoughts and business. I will, as 1 Peter 1:13 puts it in the KJV version "gird up the loins of (my) mind," which will of course fill me with nostalgic memories of former fashion crises and turn me into a blubbering mess. But once that is over, I'll be full throttle ready to follow the instructions of Peter when he said "prepare your mind for action; be self-controlled; set your hope fully on the grace to be given you when Jesus Christ is revealed. As obedient children, do not conform to the evil desires you had when you lived in ignorance. But just as he who called you is holy, so be holy in all you do" (1 Peter 1:13–15 NIV).

Until then I am feverishly slapping spackle over the holes in my mind in an effort to retain a smattering of the holiness God graciously infuses into my life day by day. Here's wishing you a wholly holy February!

For the Four-Year-Old in All of Us

March 2006

Unbelievably it's that time of year again when we pause to say, "Happy Birthday Joshua, Catherine and Christopher!" The year of the triple three threat has come and gone in the blink of an eye, and we have survived with all but our adult brains intact. What we now have jiggling around in our skulls consists of screaming fit echoes, whiffs of pee-pee puddles, enthralling tales of adventures with pretend Grandma, Bob the Builder, Santa, Robin Hood on a Nanny Deer hunt, Peter Pan and pals, hippos behind the fence, Uncle-Bret-would-know nature quests, with God, Jesus, Mary, Joseph, the Shepherds, Adam, Eve, and Daniel all squished together into tales told in simultaneous triplicate in-your-face, listen-to-me-now-this-is-serious-business-three-year-old voices, along with sweet prayers, cozy cuddles with books, and lots of hugs and giggles. Personally, I think that beats having fully functioning minds any day!

Now we're on to the Year of the Dog, and not just because the little triplets are half Chinese. Although my own daughters fourth years do not stand out in my memory, perhaps because year three sucked the few brain cells out that I had left after years one and two (see paragraph one), I seem to recall that they did morph into doggish creatures on a regular basis. First, they would whine their request (Mommmmyyyyyy!) then move on to full throttle begging (Please oh please oh PLEASE!). If that didn't work they'd ratchet it up a notch to barking a command (Mommy, DO IT RIGHT NOW, I

WANT IT!) at which time they would meet their four-year-old fate, which we lovingly named Mr. Spoon. Rarely did Mr. Spoon have to meet my daughters' bottoms. He would usually wink at them during the begging point, which tended to muzzle the bark before the first woof.

If those behaviors don't call to mind a spiritual parallel, then bless your bones, you must be a bona fide saint in the heavenlies! Or maybe I'm just bad. Either way, God loves us all, and enjoys us as much as we enjoy our children, even when Mr. Spoon needs to make an appearance.

For Satan Kickers

April 2006

What do you get when you mix a Beth Moore study called *Why Godly People Do Ungodly Things*, with a sermon series on "American Idols," then add reading *The Da Vinci Code* by Dan Brown to a poetry contest writing blitz? If you're me, which most of you aren't (let us praise the Lord for His great mercies) you get provoked to all manner of intense thought and write a strange poem.

TIME WARP TIME WARP TIME WARP TIME WARP

It is now January 2018 and I am continuing to work on revisions to this collection of Doodles for the publishing company. The strange poem that appeared here in the church newsletter was about a conversation with God that I made up. I think it was one I wrote with words I had asked family members to write on slips of paper, then I would pull out a few and attempt to put them all in a poem— one of those ways to spark a little creativity. Unfortunately, the publishing company I'm working with does not allow any kind of "quoting God", or saying He spoke to or told me something, not even speaking to my heart or whispering to my soul. Leading me is okay, but not speaking in any fashion. I've been going through these writings for the umpteenth time changing the wording when I've felt God was trying to lead me somewhere in my journey. I've probably missed some and will have to make more changes. But let me assure you, so far in my life, God has never spoken audibly to me and He has never told me to give someone else a message directly from Him. However, He has worked in my life in many specific ways to help me understand his Word and apply it to my own life. And these writings are part of His purpose for me in this world to share with others who might need some encouragement in the dailyness of life.

Since the poem that was originally in this space was in its entirety a fictional conversation with God, I couldn't figure out a way to change it to make it acceptable. I can assure you that you are not missing much. It was not one of my best poems, but it was certainly different. The message of the poem was to "fortify our offense" in the spiritual battle between good and evil. Get out there and kick Satan right between the eyeballs with the Word of God!

A strange poem, although inspirational to me, may not encourage the masses to do some Satan kicking with God's Word of truth. The main point to remember is the devil has no power to deceive us when we speak the truth back at him. He knows the truth. We'd better know it, too. Let's keep studying, praying, and kicking!

For All School-Weary Souls

May 2006

Why is it that when May rolls around, my brain clogs up like an overstuffed enchilada oozing heartburn into my soul every time I attempt an intelligent thought of my own? Is it because I secretly enjoy the spicy hustle and bustle of school ooze, more than my own boring brilliance? Or perhaps I'm way too involved in the lives of my daughters and should move away to the Swiss Alps until all research papers, book reports, and mathematical equations fade into memory, but that seems a tad excessive, even for me. Aside from rolling up into a big ball of chocolate flab for the remainder of the school year, what can I do? Well, dahlings, if you don't know the answer to that by now, you must not read this column very often, which I will pretend to ignore out of respect for myself.

It's a poem, dear reader, in honor of my favorite poet, William Wordsworth, to take our minds off the school ooze that dribbles non-stop from every corpuscle of our bodies this time of year!

Walking With Wordsworth

From Tintern Abbey to Westminster Bridge
I've walked with Wordsworth through the daffodils
And mourned for Lucy, admired Coleridge.
I've wandered lonely as a cloud o'er hills
To find his splendor in the grass to be
The best of reasons to read poetry.

And though two hundred years divide our lives
His poems speak to issues in our day.
The world that's too much with us still contrives
To steal our hearts and sell them all away.
And Child is father of the Man to be,
While searching for his immortality.

Those thoughts that often lie too deep for tears
Make reading through his works a joyful climb
Out of my routine life with all its fears
Into his world of ponderings sublime.
Strange fits of passion force me to my pen
Whenever Wordsworth's lines I read again.

I feel better now. How about you?

For Fellow Former Night Owls

June 2006

Howdy folks! It's 1:00 a.m. on prom night and I have nothing better to do than write a doodle while waiting for my daughter to come home. Unfortunately, I don't believe I am at my creative zenith at this time of day anymore. The brain waves have already waved goodnight. But that shan't (or is it shalln't or shoon't ?) stop me, because this could possibly be the only time available for such pursuits during this glorious last week of school. Well then, people, sit, stand or kneel back and enjoy the incoherent ramblings of a mother with absolutely no idea what letter of the alphabet is going to come next in this priceless (and possibly pointless) classic doodle.

First of all, I want to know why 1:00 a.m. never seemed this late when I was the one that was out being young and oblivious to all parental concern and sleep needs? Secondly, I want to know how I became a parent of teenagers so fast? I haven't gotten over toddlers yet! Plus, I was a teenager myself about five years ago. Thirdly, I want to know when my children will stop causing me to lose sleep? Is this an incurable, chronic disease that descends upon a mother as her child descends the birth canal?

Next, I would like someone to explain how come God knows what He is doing all the time and I hardly ever know anything until it is all over, and then I look back and think aha! So that's what all that messy business was about. It seems to me that if I knew what God was doing when He was doing it I could help out a little and get it done quicker. (No, I don't think that would work.)

Finally—I really, really want to see a show of hands here—does anybody else out there have a prublem with spelling! punctuation, grammarand; syntax at this time of the day/ If so, read this at 1:00 in the morning and everything will make sense. Hey! Way cool epiphany happening here! Maybe God is a night owl, too, and we just need to "read" His messages to us at the right time in order to understand them. Mercy, that was fun!

For Anyone in Search of a Brain

August 2006

Hello people! After a short, forced break from doodledom, I'm sure you are frothing at the bit to read the pearls of wisdom that a brain vacation most surely has rained down upon me. Regrettably, the doodle brain veered off its AAA plotted path to the Kuss vacation spot in the backyard and has not been heard from since. I have a sinking feeling that Eujane the dog may have mistaken it for a beloved toy and either chewed it to bits or buried it. We will know for sure in another month or so, or possibly never.

In the meantime, you will have to make due with a few random thoughts that may not be pearls, but if you string them together into your own personal pattern, they could sparkle and clink together like plastic beads that may keep you awake for a while until you decide to throw them away.

Random Thought #1 The first two paragraphs strike me as just about as random as it gets, so they will count as #1.

Random Thought #2 Why did God create ticks, fleas and mosquitoes? I'm sure my biologist husband could answer this, but I'd rather hear it from God.

Random Thought #3 Does anyone else think staying married to the same person for 28 years constitutes a miracle? How about if that person enjoys creepy crawly critters that end up on the kitchen table in empty ice cream containers at regular intervals?

Random Thought #4 Why are the Kansas City Royals such a crummy baseball team right now and why should anyone around here care? Just wait—they'll be back one of these days! (TIME WARP FROM THE FUTURE—*2015 World Series Champions!!*)

Random Thought #5 With all the scary stuff going on in the world, isn't it comforting to know God loves each one of us, He knows all our random thoughts, and He even knows all the answers, including where the dog buried my brain?

For the Overanxious Types

September 2006

Two weeks ago, I took on the dreaded job of defrosting my freezer and guess what I found! Way back in a corner, behind Bret's treasure trove of dead critters, I came across my missing brain! What a reunion we had once the August heat thawed it out and the mad rush of school starting shocked it back into working order. How it came to be in the freezer remains a mystery, but I think Eujane the dog must have had something to do with it. She has a thing for ice cubes.

Anyway, this glorious reunion came just in the nick of time. In that same week, we bought another vehicle so our college freshman (Erin) could commute to classes, and we learned that our college senior (Amy) was officially ENGAGED to be married just as soon as possible after her May graduation!! Oh, my mercies—Tizzidom has never seen the likes of the convulsive heart palpitations that overcame me with that news. I've never been the calm sort (that's Bret—he's so calm I have to check his pulse on a regular basis to make sure I'm not a widow). In fact, I am probably the most anxious person this side of a psychiatric ward you'll ever meet. Life has always been just one big "Oh land sakes! How will this ever work?" after another to me.

Fortunately, God knows this. He obviously gave me a high-strung soul for some reason, maybe to keep Bret awake. Whatever His purposes, God always provides what I need to get through it all.

The same week all that excitement occurred, I joined a new Sunday School class to study the book, *Calm My Anxious Heart* by Linda Dillow. As loony as I am at times, I know a God thing when it hits me in the face, and this is a God thing. He's going to teach me some good stuff in the next few months, so be prepared to hear about it, whether you like it or not!

I've already learned, through living with myself all these years, that my first inclination to go into a tizzy about everything is not the best response. That may seem obvious to you calm types out there, but to me it's a breakthrough into blazing clarity! Stay tuned.

For Mud Wallowers

October 2006

When last we met, I was in the midst of an anxiety attack over having two daughters in college with one getting married early next summer. I was also in the beginning stages of learning to be calm and content instead of anxious by studying the book, *Calm My Anxious Heart*. Here's what I've learned so far:

I may be a nervous, fear-driven, negative thinker by genetics and habit, but I don't have to stay that way. I can *choose* to think positively, and trust God, as Paul encouraged in Philippians 4:8-9 (NIV): "Finally brothers, whatever is true, whatever is noble, whatever is right, whatever is pure, whatever is lovely, whatever is admirable—if anything is excellent or praiseworthy—think about such things. Whatever you have learned or received or heard from me, or seen in me—put it into practice. And the God of peace will be with you." Even if it means making that choice over and over again every five minutes, that is exactly what I need to do right now in my present state.

I need to be content with who I am. God gave me this introverted, rigid, self-conscious, slightly obsessive personality for a reason. Instead of wishing I could be the fun, friendly, calm, cool and collected type, God wants me to be the best me I can be, in order to reach the people that respond to the introverted, rigid, obsessive types, bless their crazy hearts. I am God's poem. I am a rabbit, not a duck. I do not bowl or swim. I write and play with children and pray—that's all good! God has been pushing this concept at me for about ten years, so I'm getting better at it.

I really need to practice looking up at the stars. This quote from Frederick Langbridge mentioned in the book convicted me greatly— "Two men looked through prison bars. One saw mud, the other saw stars." People, I am a long-time mud gazer. For most of my life, whenever anything new, unscheduled, or even slightly out of my comfort zone came up, I wouldn't just look at the mud, I'd fling myself headfirst into the mud and wallow in all the negative what-if, I don't like it, why did this happen, and I'm doomed thoughts. After wallowing for minutes, days, months, sometimes years, I'd roll over to catch my breath and wipe the slimy gunk out of my eyes, and THEN I would look up and see the stars shining brightly down on me from God's love and perfect plan for me. Well, bless my soul! I'm determining right now to start looking up first, before I take a nosedive into the stinky pit. I'm sure for a while I'll catch myself mid-dive flailing my way back up like a cartoon character, or aiming for the trampoline on the side of the pit, but someday I'm going to do it right the first time. Then you'll see me singing and dancing, arms raised, like the girls in the Praise Team at church, only flabbier. And not so public. You'll have to sneak up on me in my rabbit hutch to see it.

For Holy Thanksgiving, Batman! Types

November 2006

Howdy folks! Here we are entering the Thanksgiving season once again, and I think I hear a couple of voices from my childhood calling.

"Holy streaking molecules of time warpity, Batman! How did we arrive back here again so soon?"

"Now, now Robin. Don't let the swift passage of time give you a runner in your tights! As newly inducted members of the Calm and God-Trusting Hearts Club, let us not dwell on the gut-wrenching PACE OF THE WEEKS AHEAD, or the even more throat-clenching BUSYNESS BEFORE AMY'S WEDDING, MERE MONTHS AWAY."

"If you say so, Batman, but it's hard to ignore all those capital letters."

"That's why we're going to take a poetic moment to meditate on the beauty of this glorious autumnal season, my young, hyper sidekick."

Debra Kuss

God's Season

When apples ripen crisp upon the tree
Kentucky lies beneath a patchwork throw.
Though colors fade, their warmth remains with me.

I long to walk the countryside and flee
The burdens that the days of summer sow,
When apples ripen crisp upon the tree.

I'll turn a corner on a trail and see
A blazing orange maple and a doe.
Though colors fade, their warmth remains with me.

I'll cross a rushing brook pollution free,
A breeze will pink my cheeks into a glow,
When apples ripen crisp upon the tree.

And when I must turn back, I'll have the key
To facing problems each new day might know.
Though colors fade, their warmth remains with me.

While every season speaks His majesty,
God's love shines like a beacon I follow,
When apples ripen crisp upon the tree.
Though colors fade, their warmth remains with me.

Have a happy, anxiety free Thanksgiving!

EPILOGUE

For Those Who Managed
to Read This Far

October 2017

This concludes the early years of Desperately Doodling Debbie. Soon after writing the last doodle in this book, I was informed that the church was paring down the monthly newsletter to just one page. It had become a behemoth of eight to ten pages and was costing way too much to print and mail out. Thus, without a chance to write one last goodbye doodle to my readers, I simply faded into the sunset for a few years. And just when life was getting more exciting than ever!

I continued writing poems and entering poetry contests, but I missed the monthly therapy of pouring out whatever blather came to mind in a column format. My new son-in-law, Chris, and his grandmother were fans of my doodles, so in 2010, Chris, a technology wizard, set me up with a blog site where I could continue my monthly ramblings. I've been online for seven years now, so if you want to read more, go to desperatelydoodlingdebbie.com.

Thank you to all who have bought this book. I hope you haven't been too warped by it.

ACKNOWLEDGEMENTS

Thank you to my family for providing rich fodder for my many Doodles over the years, and for not rolling their eyes too much when they wished I would leave them out of my angsty confessions. Special thanks to middle daughter, Erin, who just happened to be home at the right time to help me proof this book, managing to make some of my convoluted sentences less so, and helping me find parts that went missing when I either hit the wrong button, or simply forgot where on the computer something vital was hiding. Special superdeedooper thanks to my youngest, daughter, Carly, for the artwork she contributed to this book, as well as her technological skill in the formatting process. I would be banging my head against a wall and vacillating between hysterical screaming and laughing fits even now without her help.

Thank you, also, to the people at Westbow Press for helping me through the publishing process.

You can find Debbie's poetry book, Heaven and Earth, at blurb.com

About the Author

When Debra Kuss, the writer, is not doodling in desperation, or penning perspicacious poetry, her other sort-of-normal self, retired nanny Debbie, knits in spurts, reads great and not so great novels, teaches Sunday School, and hangs out with whatever part of her family (biology professor Bret, three grown daughters, three grandchildren, one bloodhound, and random fish) is available.

Printed in the United States
By Bookmasters